POETRY REV

SPRING 1998 VOLUME 88

EDITOR PETER FORBES
PRODUCTION STEPHEN TROUSSE
ADVERTISING SOPHIE JEPSON SUBSCRIPTIONS EMMA JARVIE

CONTENTS

LONDON MAGAZINE

FICTION * MEMOIRS * CRITICISM * POETRY
CINEMA * ARCHITECTURE * PHOTOGRAPHY
THEATRE * ART * MUSIC

'A fantastic magazine whose place in the history
of 20th century literary life grows ever more secure
and significant' – *William Boyd, Evening Standard*

Each issue contains over 50 pages of poems and
reviews of poetry.

Forthcoming features

Poems by Anthony Thwaite * Roger Garfitt *

Michael Hulse * Fergus Allen * George Szirtes *

A Dutch Quarter

New Czech Poetry

Michael O'Neil and Peter Bland on recent books

Subscriptions:
£28.50 p.a. (six issues) to 30 Thurloe Place, London SW7

Single copies £5.99 from discriminating bookshops

POETRY REVIEW
SUBSCRIPTIONS
Four issues including postage:

UK individuals £23
Overseas individuals £31
(all overseas delivery is by airmail)
USA individuals $56

Libraries, schools and institutions:
UK £30
Overseas £37
USA $66

Single issue £5.95 + 50p p&p (UK)

Sterling and US dollar payments only.
Eurocheques, Visa and Mastercard
payments are acceptable.

Bookshop distribution:
Password Books
Telephone 0161 953 4009

Design by Philip Lewis
Cover by Stephen Troussé
Image © Tony Stone Images

Typeset by Poetry Review.

Printed by Grillford Ltd at
26 Peverel Drive, Bletchley,
Milton Keynes MK1 1QZ
Telephone: 01908 644123

POETRY REVIEW is the magazine of the
Poetry Society. It is published quarterly
and issued free to members of the Poetry
Society. Poetry Review considers submis-
sions from non-members and members
alike. To ensure reply submissions must
be accompanied by an SAE or adequate
International Reply coupons: Poetry
Review accepts no responsibility for
contributions that are not reply paid.

Founded 24 February 1909
Charity Commissioners No: 303334
© 1998

THE POETRY SOCIETY

EDITORIAL AND BUSINESS ADDRESS:
22 BETTERTON STREET, LONDON WC2H 9BU

telephone   0171 420 9880
fax   0171 240 4818
email   poetrysoc@dial.pipex.com
website   http://www.poetrysoc.com

ISBN 1 900771 08 X
ISSN 0032 2156

Funded by
THE
ARTS
COUNCIL
OF ENGLAND

WHAT COMES NEXT AND HOW TO LIKE IT

Peter Forbes on New American Poetry

THE MUTUAL LACK of interest between British and American poetry has been notorious for decades now. Whether it is worse than in the other arts is hard to say: probably it is. In film, the novel and rock music American work is either dominant or at least part of the mix, and every now and again the slogan "The Brits are coming" gets wheeled out in the USA and it's not all hype. The Sensational new British painters and sculptors have some presence in America. But the question: How to sell British poetry in the States is one that no one has yet attempted to answer. But we can start to address the other side of the equation. The *Review* last devoted an issue to America in 1991. In retrospect it was very reliant on those few figures such as Sharon Olds and C. K. Williams who had recently made a splash here with readings.

But American poetry isn't so inaccessible. The place to start is the annual anthology, *The Best American Poetry*, published by Scribners and available here from Simon and Schuster, under the general editorship of David Lehman, who started the series in 1988. He appoints an editor for each volume – figures like Ashbery and Graham, etc have all done a stint. It is America's *Forward*, a shop window of mainstream US poetry.

The introductions to the *Best American Poetry* make fascinating reading. For instance, they suggest that everything that happens here seems to happen there – and this isn't the usual Anglo aping of US fads. Given the decoupled nature of the two poetries it is a genuine cultural parallelism. There is a "poetry boom" in America, with a National Poetry Month, a ra ra lobby pointing to recent Nobel Prize winners and a general buoyancy, and, in the opposite camp, a grumpy tendency (Richard Howard called National Poetry Month "the worst thing to have happened to poetry since the advent of the

> There is a "poetry boom" in America, with a ra ra lobby pointing to recent Nobel Prize winners and a general buoyancy, and, in the opposite camp, a grumpy tendency (Richard Howard called National Poetry Month "the worst thing to have happened to poetry since the advent of the camera and the internal combustion engine").

camera and the internal combustion engine").

In this issue Stephen Burt identifies a new tendency in the latest generation. This mostly hasn't filtered through into the *Best American Poetry* yet but there is still a strong, identifiable mood in the anthologies of the last few years. The most influential figures are Stephen Dobyns and James Tate and behind them all to some degree lies Ashbery. Somewhere along the line surrealism has fused with American expansiveness to create a poetry which, at its best, is exhilarating.

America is also always a ripe field for making rediscoveries. John Greening makes the case for some neglected figures in his piece in this issue. A few others well worth consideration by an English publisher include Gwendolyn Brooks, the *doyenne* of Black American women poets, a poet still anthologised but out of print here in volume form. Randall Jarrell was once published by Faber and is now famous mainly as a critic but he wrote perhaps the best poems of the Second World War and ought to be read. In our last American issue James Wood made a case for Howard Nemerov, then still alive. Somehow, Nemerov has never caught on over here (he is published by Chicago University Press) but his work is an inexhaustible compendium of mid-20th century life, occasionally perhaps too folksy in the Frost manner, but at his best he is a great civic poet. Adrienne Rich is well-known enough here but in a rather reductive way; the range of her work exceeds the bounds of the stereotype that she was a gifted formalist ('Aunt Jennifer's Tigers') who discovered free form and became radical in the '70s.

There is still some way to go before English and American poetries are read with equal ease and enthusiasm on both sides but the climate seems more propitious than for many years.

Shearing Away

STEPHEN BURT DEFINES THE STYLE OF A NEW GENERATION
OF AMERICAN POETS: ELLIPTICISM

STEPHEN DOBYNS' BEST poem shows a man and dog staring into a refrigerator at dawn, looking for "answers to what comes next, and how to like it". Young American poets seeking such answers face an exciting, if a cluttered, field. James Merrill is no longer with us (though his followers are); John Ashbery is everywhere, and is perhaps now too prolific; and Jorie Graham has become an unavoidable presence in other people's styles, partly because she teaches at Iowa and gets lots of press, but mostly because her cinematic, intellective *The End of Beauty* (1987) established her as her generation's best poet. The most exciting younger poets have read Graham and do not imitate her; they share goals and tones and attitudes, and the best way to explain what they share is, I fear, to coin a term for a school.* I therefore introduce the Elliptical Poets. I made up the school, but all the books are real; most still await UK publishers.

Elliptical Poets are always hinting, punning or swerving away from a never-quite-unfolded backstory; they are easier to process in parts than in wholes. Elliptics seek the authority of the rebellious; they want to challenge their readers, violate decorum, surprise or explode assumptions about what belongs in a poem, or what matters in life, and to do so while meeting traditional lyric goals. Their favorite attitudes are desperately extravagant, or tough-guy terse, or defiantly childish: they don't believe in, or seek, a judicious tone. Elliptical poets like insistent, bravura forms, and forms with repetends — sestinas, pantoums, or fantasias on single words, like Liam Rector's 'Saxophone':

> You and I, our money. Their money.
> Our pleasure and fist full of money.
> Laughter over money, serious money,
> over money. Too much, too little,
> fluid money. The saxophone, color of wheat,
> purchased through Hock Shop money, saxophone
> splitting the night, our air, blowing money.

Rector's *The Sorrow of Architecture* (1984) may be the first Elliptical book. Rector's anger stems

from his Brechtian interest in work, debt and wages, in "the ongoing circulation / Of art and money... the hunger, // The hunt, the eat". He may have invented the fractured sestina forms that pervade poems like 'Driving November', a three-page work with the proportionate strength of a crime-spree film:

> We are driving November we turned
> October several towns back. We applaud
> the passing of all that is innocent we inherit
> the road as it is here. You speak of habit
> as if things do not change I speak
> of sweet repetition. We are driving November, from
> harm.

Ellipticals love poems that declare "I am X, I am Y, I am Z", where X, Y and Z are incompatible things. Mark Levine, who specializes in such poems, also shares Rector's interests in money, locality and work. Levine's debut *Debt* (1993) is Ellipticism at its most aggressive, rife with allusion and disillusion. His punky 'Work Song' proves him Berryman's legatee:

> I am Henri, mouth full of soda crackers.
> I live in Toulouse, which is a piece of cardboard.
> Summers the Mayor paints it blue, we fish in it.
> Winters we skate on it. Children are always
> drowning or fallling through cracks. Parents are
> distraught
> but get over it. It's easy to replace a child.
> Like my parents' child, Henri.

Elliptical poets create inversions, homages, take-offs on old or "classic" poems; they also adapt old subgenres — aubade, elegy, verse-letter, and especially ode. Almost all write good prose poems. Lucie Brock-Broido is the most ambitious, most tradition-conscious Elliptical. Her *The Master Letters* (1995) quarries Dickinson, Donne, *Romeo and Juliet*, exclaims "I am angel, addict, catherine wheel – a piece of work / On fire"; specifies, "At your feet I am a shoemaker's apprentice, / Toxic in a long

*My thanks to Douglas Wolk for telling me to invent a school, and to Jessica Bennett and Monica Youn for suggestions.

day of fumes"; entitles a poem 'You Can't Always Get What You Want', and opens it with backtalk from *Lolita*: "Light of your loins – I have been to the ruins & come back with art". Her prose poems boast menageries of similes – "senseless as crates of fish stacked glimmering, one-eyed & blank, one atop the other of them"; the best of her many personae may be Anne Boleyn, in a poem called (after Wyatt) 'And Wylde for to Hold':

Lack of water, lack of light,
Lack of heat, lack of bedding, I should go

On this way forever; it is
        my wont to go.
Tonight – the wind will
be high in its scaffolding,

On the strength. I will
        listen for its habit
Especially about the
        throat like an
        Elizabethan cuff

At the crude nest of the
        mouth. Our bed
Will be lined with shred-
ded bark from sycamore
        & hair.

Let them lie broad awake
in their nest, scissoring.
None will fly.

Ellipticals caress the technical; there is, as Rebecca Reynolds puts it, "less / she can touch now / that isn't technical and reluctant". They mix their affections with alienations. Susan Wheeler's *Smokes* (1998) presents her sometimes as a movie star, sometimes as a "hapless stand-in scripter" with an "impedimented personality", fleeing or seeking love or fame. She makes leaps from low to high diction; likes to interrupt herself; writes "I am X, I am Y" poems; and mixes up old high allusions with TV and Barbies. Her talent lies in her kidnapping of familiar forms, as in 'Shanked on the Red Bed' (an update, perhaps, of MacNeice's 'Bagpipe Music'):

The century was breaking and the blame was on
        default,
The smallest mammal redolent of what was in the
        vault,

The screeches shrill, the ink-lines full of interbred
        regret –
When I walked out to look for you the toad had left
        his net.

The discourse flamed, the jurors sang, the lapdog
        strained his leash –
When I went forth to have you found the tenured
        took the beach
With dolloped hair and jangled nerves, without a
        jacking clue,
While all around the clacking sound of polished
        woodblocks blew.

August Kleinzahler is Elliptical in his all-inclusiveness, his casual refusals of authority, his jarring jumps from elevation to slang. Kleinzahler's wry, Californian cadences can encompass anything he sees or hears – the sun from a plane, headlines, Thom Gunn, dogwoods, crisps, DTs. A ballet he watches prompts 'Sapphics in Traffic', which begins, "Festinating rhythm's bothered her axis"; where Larkin wrote 'Lines on a Young Lady's Photograph Album', Kleinzahler writes the semi-rhymed, half-nostalgic quatrains of 'Ruined Histories':

Ah, Little Girl Destiny, it's sprung a leak
and the margins are bleeding themselves away.
You and I and the vase and stars won't stay still.
Wild, wild, wild – kudzu's choked the topiary.

Looks like your history is about to turn
random and brutal, much as an inch of soil or
        duchy.
Not at all that curious hybrid you had in mind.
Jane Austen, high-tech and a measure of Mom.

Like the Eliot of 'Prufrock', or the Berryman of *The Dream Songs*, the Ellipticals delete their transitions: one thought, one impression, tailgates another. C. D. Wright is expert at laying down a series of hints, or residues, of experience, making readers discover what happened. Wright began publishing in the late 1970s, but her best books are recent: her first fully Elliptical work is *String Light* (1991), full of detailed tenderness for, and scorched regret about, her native Arkansas. She, too, has a rebellious "I" poem, 'Personals':

> In this humidity I make repairs by night. I'm not one
> among many who saw Monroe's face
> in the moon. I go blank looking at that face.
> If I could afford it I'd live in hotels. I won awards
> in spelling and the Australian crawl. Long long ago.
> Grandmother married a man named Ivan. The men
> called him
> Eve. Stranger, to tell the truth, in
> dog years I am up there.

Wright's technique of hinting allows her in *Tremble* (1996) to make terse, radiant sketches of bodily, erotic histories, 'Key Episodes from an Earthly Life': the poem of that name begins "As surely as there are crumbs on the lips / of the blind I came for a reason". It ends:

> Around this time of year   especially evening
> I love everything   I sold enough eggs
>
> To buy a new dress   I watched him drink the juice
> Of our beets   And render the light liquid
>
> I came to talk you into physical splendor
> I do not wish to speak to your machine

Thylias Moss is Ellipticism at its most tonally risky, and socially conscious: her registers include Blakean outrage, African-American preaching cadences, and the disarming backtalk of kids. Moss swerves between wisecracks and credos: her uneasy speakers, girls and adults, ground their defiance in local events, as in 'When I Was 'Bout Ten We Didn't Play Baseball':

> It's hot. We might
> sleep on the porch. Next year we really will have it
> screened so we won't ever have to respect mosquitos
> again. I listen to all the emergencies,
> sirens of course, the Cadillac horns of the wedding, a
> mother
> new to the area calling home her children
> forgetting not to call the names of the ones who
> don't

come home anymore on nights like these when all it
> has to be
> is summer and they're cared for better. The heat does
> hug.
> It isn't shy and proper. My mother wouldn't want
> me
> to play with it.

Moss favors jangly linebreaks and swift tonal shifts, Kleinzahler his slang-slinging, Brock-Broido her extravagance, because these poets want to make poems as volatile as real life. So do their peers. Most Ellipticals are between 30 and 50, and found their real styles after 1986. If they have a geographical center, it's New York City (though several have taught, or studied, at the University of Michigan). Ellipticals invoke, as precedents, Dickinson, Berryman, Ashbery, sometimes Auden; they read *New American Writing, Denver Quarterly, Conjunctions, Parnassus, Boston Review*. All want to convey both metaphysical challenge, and recognizable, seen or tasted, detail. Ellipticism rejects: poems written in order to demonstrate theories; prettiness as its own end; slogans; mysticism; and straight-up narrative. Ellipticals are uneasy about (less often, hostile to) inherited elites and privileges, but they are not populists, and won't write down to, or connect the dots for, their readers; their difficulty conveys respect.

Time will find and polish the best Elliptical verse, as it has with prevailing styles from the Tribe of Ben to the allies of Auden. I wish I had space to quote from the bedazzled, lyrical prose poet Killarney Clary; Forrest Gander's careful sequences; Karen Volkman's exceptional, varied debut *Crash's Law*; April Bernard's jittery *Blackbird Bye Bye*; Rebecca Reynolds' first book, *Daughter of the Hangnail*; the comic, tender, botanizings of Alice Fulton; and the Ellipticals' overseas counterparts, Australia's John Tranter, who often visits the USA, and Britain's Mark Ford. For now, these uneasy, *echt* contemporary, difficult American poets have written a heap of at-least-pretty-good poems. Vaunting or angry, precise but not pedantic, hip but rarely jaded, they are in all the best (and a few worse) senses, what comes next.

ELLIPTICIST READING LIST
(* denotes books available from UK publishers)

Lucie Brock-Broido, *The Master Letters* (Knopf, 1995)
Killarney Clary, *Who Whispered Near Me* (Bloodaxe, 1993)*

Jorie Graham, *The Dream of the Unified Field: Selected Poems* (Carcanet, 1996)*

August Kleinzahler, *Red Sauce, Whiskey and Snow* (Faber, 1995)*

Mark Levine, *Debt* (Norton, 1993)

Thylias Moss, *Small Congregations* (Ecco, 1995)

Liam Rector, *The Sorrow of Architecture* (Dragon Gate, 1984)

Liam Rector, *American Prodigal* (Story Line Press, 1994)

Susan Wheeler, *Smokes* (Four Way Books, 1998)

C.D. Wright, *String Light* (University of Georgia Press, 1991)

C.D.Wright, *Tremble* (Ecco, 1996)

JAMES TATE
MY PRIVATE TASMANIA

has never been discovered,
is thought to be the source of all fire,
is a pigpen for the soul,
changes its shape and location
when you try to think of it.
It smells like a funeral parlor
full of orchids and makes you
want to run for your life.
And at the same time it's sexual,
salacious, creating a terrible hunger.
My Tasmania conceals beneath her
raven-black apron hundreds of
unknown species of wild pigs.
It rocks in the wind at night
and hums a beautiful melody.
Even the birds can't sleep
and begin to sing extinct songs.
Snakes are counting their worry beads.
I'm walking in circles,
getting closer and closer.
Walls of the coalmine
that is my head
begin to cave-in, crashing
in huge chunks to the floor,
shocking the bats out of their dreams
and the rats out of gnawing
on one another. Closer, I said,
I must be getting closer.
The smell of rotting flesh
was gagging me. I couldn't see
through the smoke and haze.
I stop circling, begin to laugh.
My mother says, "Jimmy, please
stop laughing, you're frightening us".

MARK LEVINE
ENOLA GAY

I

It is many years after the fact.
I sent a squad to gather data
from the sticky asphalt, and they
are far away and very quiet. I do
wish I had not surrendered my wings.
I'm all out of seed.

And then through the pale red smoke of daybreak
I enter the garden – garden choked to its seams
with weeds and coiled roots and vines lurching
through the polished rose pebbles to the polished sky.
Can you hear the garden growing? Can you hear its motor?

Can you hear the crystal voices trapped beneath the growing?

Queen of the skies, pour forth your obsessing wrath!

II

They're having a clam-bake. With corn-on-the-cob.
With corn bread and clam juice and corn starch and clam skins.

They're having a clam-bake. They're baking my clams.
They're baking the clams pried from my steaming pond.

They're squeezing the lemon and biting the rinds.
They're plying the fire with red-veined kindling

snapped from the white depths of the powdery grove.
They're burning the kindling. They're baking. They're dwindling.

Their spines are singing. Their hooves splashed with fat.
They grow very small in the very red garden.

Cabbage at moonrise? Cabbage and air?
A mattress and a Jew's-harp and a vulgar stutter?

This year the trade-winds taste like butter,
butter and hunger, fear and sweet rain.

III

We are outfitted with small lacquered panels
whose blinking lights describe the skittish movements
of other captives. My screen is frozen and too sad to play.
I choose the Thimble, you choose the Horse, Mother the Shoe.
The Holy Son will drag behind him the Steam Iron.
And the black man? The black man is studying us

from his shady perch above the electrical storm,
his finger limp on the solemn device,
clinking "Yellow. Yellow. Yellow. Yellow".
He sure do play a pretty violin.
I transmitted a coarsely graven prayer
and disappeared into the moist and comely

Oriental air.
Thence to tame my friend the broken bear.

IV

I am with child. With child again.
This time it's a child. This time it's a secret.

Shhh. The two of us; the two of us and the sky.
At night I feel you whispering to me from your pouch,

whispering angrily of the angry sky.
The sky is your father. So am I –

your father and mother and severest mascot.
How ghostly your soul. I can tell by squinting.

I can tell by gazing with a mother's cruel black eyes
at your illuminated genes – genes spread out like spikes

in the star-heavy sky.
It's marvelous to be big. Big with the child-King.

How best I prepare you for your somber birthright?
How best I stitch the secret on your slumbering black skin?

V

There stands a house under the mountain
of the world. Its floors are coal.
Its walls are hung with skins. Its dangling lamps
divide the obscene birds from the birds of the horizon.

There stands a house. Its horns are hewn
from stone and dying trees and wound with roots
seized from the polar garden. They are horns of love
and like the scalps of love they will be ground into sanctified

explosive dust. Hear the bitter engines whine.
Hear the roll of royal dice.
Snake-eyes again. Snake-eyes in our open throats
over the Kingdom's island-splotched sea.

Is it he we retrieve from the vaporized bunker?
He that is willing? He that empties the jungles?

— Yes; if the angry hammer agrees.
And I lead him for a stroll in the clay pits at dusk.
a stroll with the viper I was taught to desire, he
with the magic instrument, he with the pierced wings, he in fancy,

he in fact. *The fact remains.*
Later we paused for a good cry and felt better.
I took a wrong turn and slid by candlelight
into the orphanage and faced the hero

in his cockpit. Here was no Negro.
His foot lay lodged in the barnacled steel trap.
He pecked at his ankle like a starved sea bird
until his teeth grew very tired.

Where can I drop you, he says.
Downtown Sumer, says I.

JORIE GRAHAM
TWO DAYS (5/2/97-5/3/97)

Full moon; lays his hand
onto her throat, into his mouth
takes her whole ear.

Noon: this pen hovers
over this empty page. One is
free to forget.

Noon. The gate fills to
its edges with the two sides of
opening. Move.

Noon. Regardless of
the gate, buds open all around,
stare at each other.

Noon: evaporation is taking
place.

Full moon: your body before me
a nameless hill.
I am not seeking altitude.

Full moon: seeing, being seen;
the cold lies in us all night long.
In one spot most especially.

Noon: we push until
like a third party
matter rages between us.

Noon: pushes us
into the midst to where
Spring stops.

Noon: pushes us
to where a crown emerges and begins to lower
all round our bodies
tiny tips of buds.

Noon: then even the buds push out
into this emptiness.

Noon. The only heaven plays and leaps.

Dusk, with its downslope,
a bride, and one above her
all shivering of mind.

Late dusk: a communication
between what exists and what
is visible (that shore) (who knows

what can be said) –

Full moon:
lays his hands onto her throat, into his mouth
takes her whole ear.

"Not Art at All"

by Carol Rumens

Exchanging Hats:
Elizabeth Bishop's Paintings
Edited & Introduced by William Benton
Carcanet £19.95
ISBN 1 85754 338 6

ELIZABETH BISHOP'S PAINTINGS were exhibited for the first time early in 1993, in Key West. The initiative came from the poet and artist William Benton, who had admired Bishop's work from the dust-jackets she had designed for three of her American publications and sus-pected there was more. Bishop was completely unknown to the "art-world", and many of the originals proved hard to track down. (Benton gives a delightful account of his detective-work, often among characters who might have lived happily in Bishop's poems.) Around 40 art-works, including sketches

Fountain (undated) pen and ink
(Collection of Loren MacIver)

and Cornell-type constructions were finally brought to light, and are reproduced in *Exchanging Hats*, with a compendium of quotes-on-art by the poet. The volume is a pleasure in its own right, and essential gazing for anyone interested in the poetry.

Though her taste in modern art was sophisti-cated (Schwitters, Ernst, Klee, etc.) there is no sense of straining for achievement in Bishop's own picture-making. It is as unpretentious, tactful and charming as her letter-writing. (The paintings too, were often meant for friends, and some bear cryptic inscriptions.) Bishop took it as the highest praise when Randall Jarrell compared her poetry to the work of Vermeer. But she insisted of her pictures: "They are not art – NOT ART AT ALL". She often worked on cheap paper, invariably small poem-sized sheets. The 12 paintings provided by Vassar College were so fragile they looked to Benton "like pressed butterflies".

Very rarely, it seems that a poem and a picture share an identical source: see the poem 'Sleeping on the Ceiling' (*North and South*) and the painting 'Chandelier', though the latter chastely eschews metaphor (ceiling as park-square, lamp as tree). Another pair that makes for interesting comparison are the undated landscape 'Nova Scotia' and 'Poem' (*Geography III*). The latter describes, in tender, intricately searching detail, an impressionistic miniature painted by "Great Uncle George": it depict low hills, elms, cows ("Two brush-strokes each, but confidently cows"), geese, a wispy church steeple and a barn ("titanium white, one dab"). While registering the changes in the scene since Uncle George's days, 'Poem' rejoices in the jolt of recognition: "Heavens, I know this place!" Could Bishop's 'Nova Scotia' record the impulse to paint her version of that miniature? Conifers have replaced the elms. But there is a white barn and a church, though the church has a solid-looking cupola, rather than a wispy spire; there are the same low hills. Another cross-current of recogni-tion thrills into life.

But 'Sestina' is the poem brought most frequently to mind. Her interiors are rosy with lamps, fireplaces, kettles and above all stoves, the latter emblazoned with such names as Fancy, Ideal, Magico. Glimpses of the child's drawing of a "rigid house" occur in several exteriors of buildings, where the strokes, though far from rigid, are effective in creating (solidity and unchallenged presence.

Flowers are another favourite subject. A stanza from the Robert Lowell elegy, 'North Haven', gives something of the vivid precision of the paintings: ("Hawkweed still burning, Daisies pied, Eyebright/ the fragrant Bedstraw's incandescent stars / and more, returned, to paint the meadows with delight".) There are a few figure-paintings, of rather doll-like females, but, surprisingly, no birds or animals, and nothing as surreal as the Man-Moth or the gentleman of Shallot. Her fascination with semi-states and mixed identities, including mirror images and inversions, may be detected only in a tendency to mix indoors and outdoors elements: a view of the sea through a porthole, a flowery field through a doorway, and all those jars and vases of flowers. Bishop's painterly hat was a sun-bonnet. But the charm is never overdone. Even when she paints her "patented slot machine" for producing dreams, it looks like a dowdy suitcase, with a curious diagram of mechanical innards. She may be more of an explorer in her poetry than in her artwork, but the same imperative, of scrupulous observation, underwrites them both.

KENNETH KOCH
CURRENCY

In the Fifties, Western Europe was the place
That had just been through a war. The currencies were wobbly.
A run-down American student could live like Wallace Stevens
Among the moguls of Hartford. This was helpful for poetry
If bad for a lot else. Not many French apartments had bathrooms,
Almost none refrigerators. One went to the public baths and looked out
The already steamed-up windows at the city.
I sat around a lot in Montparnasse
Cafés – you know them, the Select, the Dôme, and
The Rotonde. The Rotonde those days stayed open
All night. The old-fashioned French coffee machine was steaming.
It gave off an awful and awfully exciting smell.
The Surrealists were aging, like the paper of their books
Le paysan de Paris and Les malheurs des immortels
Above – up there – the river is winding. The museum is full of busts
Its large paintings are like days.
A friend was foreign and far away.
Everyone understands these things but no one is looking.
The fire escapes are in New York with everyone else.
Important here is to get my foot on the street
Before the car gets there. From the asphalt gas and steam not going up.
However there is a book store on the rue de Rennes.
Its French books are very cheap.
A book costs hardly more than a postcard in the United States.
This situation is temporary. Meanwhile I am becoming well-read
In modern French poetry. I also read La Chanson de Roland translated into Modern French
And Virgil's Eclogues and his Georgics translated into French.
They seem to make more sense to me than in English.
I find it in the air as well as in Max Jacob,
In Jouve and in de Montherlant. Surrealism is bouquet to these arrogated French tables,
Who thinks about these things.
I am away from ghostly and boasting New York.

In the bookstore I meet Henri Michaux. The kind man who owns the bookstore introduces
me to him

He thinks we may both like it
I more than Henri Michaux. I like it.
I am nervous I am some kind of phantom.
No don't buy the Larousse buy this a truly serious dictionary a man under the sidewalk in
his papery dusty crowded store says to me

But I am not that scholarly American
I am learning from Paris's streets to lead a life without consequence
But isn't that a life of consequence?
It is not very often that I get around to love-making
Not in this first early year.
Sexual passion and excitement are more interesting to me when I am older.
They interested me every year.
I am not studying this but Je t'aime and je vais jouir
I'm learning French phrases but I feel mystified and off to the side
I notice her long thin arms she wants to be an airline stewardess
If I held on long enough I'd be perhaps somewhat "French"
I want to be famous amidst the prose of everyday existence
In fact this year I don't care about fame
I have never cared about it I just want to be delighted and I'm envious
I want to be part of that enormous cake over there
That is a monument being wheeled down les Champs Elysées
I am daft about Paris's white sidewalks
Everything I have read and done since then
Is not more real. I wrote I completely forget what.
One friend said this version (#2) is "more abstract" than this (1st) one. I said Thank you.
Michaux was pleasant with me, and witty.
Invisible the monstrous sufferer of his poetry
Whereas my overexcited feeling is all too evident.
I am twenty-five years old and in good health sleeping
I'm sitting in a smoky restaurant
Thanksgiving Day Sixth Arrondissement I was not eating turkey
Or cranberry sauce but some petits suisses
These are very petits but are they suisses in what ways are they suisses
The conversation's booming around me
I feel lost in this breaking ocean of French happiness-inducing culinary indulgence
These fat bourgeois I am a thin bourgeois only because I am twenty-five
Giacometti is sitting drinking at the Dôme. He is with his followers.
I have a bicycle. I try but I can't hear one word that Giacometti says.
How long ago is it that I started to "dream in French"? Two months.
I want to be something else. I keep listening.
Life isn't infinite.

Now it may seem infinite but it isn't infinite.
Minor ailments don't interfere with my struggle to become French.
I will never become French.
I like too much to be American. Also partly French.
Jean Cocteau equals Juan Gris. They even have, almost, the same name.
Birds ce sont les oiseaux.
Here I am in Paris being miserably lonely. All the same.
All the same even Amadis de Gaul knew when it was time to go home.
When he had conquered his enemies.
I have not yet conquered France.
By the time I get close to it I think death may have conquered me.
My first "moment" on French soil which is the soil of Normandy
The ship the Degrasse lands and I put down my foot
On some sparsely grown grass mud that leads up to the platform where the train
Is that will be taking me to Paris
To Montparnasse its beds are its streets
Its pillows the cafés. I am streetless in the Hotel de Fleurus
Then I came down from there.
My mail is at American Express.
I have a friend who will not be my friend for very long.
And many, unknown, I have yet to meet.
What will it matter? It matters that I am not alone.
It matters that someone agrees
And that there are walls like energy.
I am unaware of a lot that has gone on here – the herding of the Jews
Into railroad cars, to Belsen.
I read Max Jacob "La rue Ravignan" in
Le cornet à des with its conclusion "c'est toi, Dostoievski"
In the road I pick up leaves in the street I pick up books
Max Jacob who had long ago proofread the last page of his *The Central Laboratory*
Is dead, killed by the Nazis.
Now Larry like a clown down the street
It's extremely late and Nell we three meet
And drink coffee
It tastes like dirt or metal, hot and steaming, like the whole world that's coming to be,
The coffee of our lives, the strong and bitter café de nos vies.
The yellow and pink lines come marching down the boulevard Montparnasse
We can pay for the coffee so we have the dawn.

MARK DOTY
AMERICAN SUBLIME

Closing time at the Athenaeum,
but our visitor bat
– who knows how he got in –

seems intent on staying the night;
our waving arms, a rolled Times,
the janitor's broom haven't phased him a bit.

In flits and starts he swoops
in crazy eights from cornice to
pilaster, from chandelier to book-

shelf top, from finial to plaster-
work to pediment, and seems
especially to like the vast

painting he skims like a pond,
a huge Bierstadt prospect
of Yosemite, a billboard

for immensity. The painter's
out to convince, and correct
our sense of scale: grandeur

meant not to diminish but
enlarge, as the eye hurries
up that great cleft

dome of rock, and above
it hazy light, light made material,
the crown of all this glory, a suffused

atmosphere intended to mean
intensely. Our friendly bat
doesn't stop to look, careening

above this antique ad
for nature as though he owned
it, and these books and music stands

and brass easels which display
last century's exotica
leaning back, labeled, heavily framed.

He brushes the canvas
with a velvety dust-rag wing
on his flight from dome to case-

ment, pausing to rest – a beat –
on that bust of, who is it,
Emerson? And now we

visitors, though we've all enjoyed
the unexpected fluttery show,
give up. Time to go home.

Where did we park?
Dim the lamps. Last glance:
bat and Bierstadt all in the dark.

Nothing. No, there he is! Flying,
just visible in the faint signal
glow of the exit sign:

our little hero still
circumambulating the gloss of oil,
the polished pools and waterfall, our rocks
                                    and rills.

LOUISE GLÜCK
VOID

I figured out why you won't buy furniture.
You won't buy furniture because you're depressed.

I'll tell you what's wrong with you: you're not
gregarious. You should
look at yourself; the only time you're totally happy
is when you cut up a chicken.

Why can't we talk about what I want to talk about?
Why do you always change the subject?

You hurt my feelings. I do *not* mistake
reiteration for analysis.

You should take one of those chemicals,
maybe you'd write more.
Maybe you have some kind of void syndrome.

You know why you cook? Because
you like control. A person who cooks is a person who likes
to create debt.

Actual people! Actual human beings
sitting on our chairs in our living room!
I'll tell you what: I'll learn
bridge.

Don't think of them as guests, think of them
as extra chickens. You'd like it.
If we had more furniture
you'd have more control.

MICHAEL DONAGHY
BLACK ICE AND RAIN

Psalms 6.6

Can I come in? I saw you slip away.
Hors d'oeuvres depress you, don't they? They do me.
And cocktails, jokes . . . such dutiful abandon.
Where the faithful observe immovable feasts
– boat races, birthdays, marriages, martyrdoms –
we're summoned to our lonely ceremonies anytime:
B minor, the mouldiness of an old encyclopaedia,
the tinny sun snapping off the playground swings,
these are, though we can't know this, scheduled
to arrive that minute of the hour, hour of the day,
day of every year. Again, regular as brickwork,
comes the time the nurse jots on your chart
before she pulls the sheet across your face. Just so,
the past falls open anywhere – even sitting here with you.

Sorry. You remind me of a girl I knew.
I met her at a party much like this, but louder, younger,
the bass so fat, the night so sticky you could drown.
We shouted art at each other over soul
and cold beer in the crowded kitchen and I, at least,
was halfway to a kiss when she slipped
her arm around her friend.
I worked at liking him, and it took work,
and it never got any easier being harmless,
but we danced that night like a 3 way game of chess
and sang to Curtis Mayfield pumped so loud
that when I drove them home they could hardly
whisper to invite me up.

Their black walls smirked with Jesus on black velvet
– Jesus, Elvis, Mexican skeletons, big eyed Virgins,
Rodin's hands clasped in chocolate prayer –
an attitude of decor, not like this room of yours.
A bottle opened – tequila with a cringe of worm –
and she watched me.
Lighting a meltdown of Paschal candles,
she watched me. He poured the drinks rasping
We're seriously into cultural detritus. At which, at last,
she smiled. Ice cubes cracked. The worm sank in my glass.

And all that long year we were joined at the hip.

I never heard them laugh. They had,
instead, this tic of scratching quotes in air –
like frightened mimes inside their box of style,
that first class carriage from whose bright window
I watched the suburbs of my life recede.
                    Exactly one year on she let me kiss her – once –
her mouth wine-chilled, my tongue a clumsy guest,
and after that the invitations dwindled.
By Christmas we were strangers. It was chance
I heard about the crash. He died at once.
Black ice and rain, they said. No news of her.
I can't remember why I didn't write.
Perhaps I thought she'd sold the flat and left.

Some nights midway to sleep I'm six years old.
Downstairs it's New Year's Eve. Drink and shrieks.
But my mother's lit the luminous plastic Jesus
to watch me through the night which is why
I've got my pillow wrapped around my head.
I never hear the door. And when she speaks,
her thick-tongued anger rearing like a beast,
I feel my hot piss spreading through the sheets.
But when I wake, grown up, it's only sweat.
But if I dream, I bleed. A briar crown,
a fist prized open wide, a steadied nail,
a hammer swinging down – the past falls open
anywhere . . .
                    Ash Wednesday evening.
Driving by, I saw her lights were on.
I noticed both their names still on the buzzer
and when I rang I heard her voice. *Come in –*
            her nose was broken, her front teeth gone,
a rosary was twisted round her fists –
            – *Come in. I've been saying a novena.*
Inside, each crucifix and candle shone
transfigured in her chrysalis of grief.
She spoke about the crash, how she'd been driving,
how they had to cut her from the wreck . . .
and then she slipped and called me by his name.

Of those next hours I remember most

the silences between her sobs, the rain
against the skylight slowly weakening
to silence, silence brimming into sleep and dawn.
Then, having lain at last all night beside her,
having searched at last that black walled room,
the last unopened chamber of my heart,
and found there neither pity nor desire
but a collection of religious kitsch,
I inched my arm from under her and left.

       Since then, the calmest voice contains her cry
just within the range of human hearing
and where I've hoped to hear my name gasped out
from cradle, love bed, death bed, there instead
I catch her voice, her broken lisp, his name.
       Since then, each night contains all others,
nested mirror-within-mirror, stretching back from then
to here and now, this party, this room, this bed,
where, in another life, we might have kissed.
Thank you, friend, for showing me your things
you have exquisite taste – but let's rejoin your guests
who must by now be wondering where you've gone.

ALICE FRIMAN
HUNGER

All love has the tug of the first nipple.
Go to Rome. Romulus and Remus
still patty-cake in the shade of a hairy teat
even in public. Soon typewriters will be obsolete
but never that. It's the gold chain
back to the breast pocket, love's first taste
without the sting of salt: rosebud fresh
and wet in the mouth.

The Hawaiians used to say
spirits leave the body through the inner angle
of the eye and return through the feet,
struggling up the body's dark passages.
But I say, love – the singing "Ahhhh"
every tongue depressor's looking for –
makes a home inside the mouth and stays there.
That's why at birth the mouth is readied,

swabbed clean as a foyer. What else
is man's facial hair but welcome mat for more?
A broom sweeping up around love's entrance.

Even at the end, under oxygen,
eyes shut, fingers no more than dried leaves
whispering to the sheets, the mouth
sucking, sucking on the exhausted tongue.

BILLY COLLINS
BERMUDA

When we walk down the bleached-out wooden stairs
to the beach and lie on our backs
on the blue and white chaises
near the edge of the water
on this dot in the atlas,
this single button on the blazer of the sea,
we come about as close
as a man and a woman can
to doing nothing.

All morning long we watch the clouds
roll overhead
or close our eyes and do the lazy
back and forth of talk,
our voices flattened by the drone of surf,
our words tumbling oddly in the wind.

It's Good Friday here, hundreds of miles
from any mass of land,
thousands from Calvary.
Wild hibiscus twists along the roadsides,
the yellow-breasted bird sings its own name,
and all the stores are closed
because today is the day to make hot cross buns
and fly kites from the beaches –
to eat the sweet cross,
to hold the cross in the sky by a spool.

The white sand keeps heating up
and one of us points out the snout of a pig
on the horizon, and higher up
a gaping alligator is about to eat
a smaller cloud.
See how that one is a giant head,
like the devil wearing glasses
you say, but my eyes are shut against the sun
and I only hear your words,
softened and warped by the sea breeze,

telling me how the head is changing into a bicycle,
the high-wheel kind on playing cards,
while the sea rushes in, falls back –
marbles pouring endlessly onto a marble floor –

and the two of us so blessedly calm
as if this were not our only life,
just one in a series, charms on a bracelet,
as if every day we were not running
like these solitary runners on the beach
toward a darkness without shape
or waves, crosses or clouds,

as if one of us is not likely to get there first
leaving the other behind,
castaway on an island where
there are no pink houses with blue shutters,
no plum-colored ones trimmed in cream,
no offshore reef to burst the waves into foam,
and no familiar, languid words being bent in the wind.

DICK ALLEN

ALTHOUGH THE TEMPORAL IS BEAUTIFUL

No one prefers a halfway finished thing,
An apple left half-eaten on the plate,
The lukewarm eddy between love and hate,
A ball thrown lightly, a half-hearted swing.

When everything is neither here nor there,
What can I praise and what can I forgive?
All furniture is merely decorative,
The ballerina never floats on air.

I half-reformed my life. It fell apart.
You can't repair a thing left half-complete.
The half-constructed building down the street
Is not a case of ruin become art.

Houses left half-painted, days that can't decide
If anything but gray is right for us,
In their neglect become contemptuous:
We trusted them, and then they went and lied.

Still even worse are those who chat up fame,
Who love intending, but who work offhand.
They roll in plans like puppies roll in sand,
And when they quit halfway, the world's to blame.

The wars we hate most are the wars half-fought.
Left to themselves, they tanktread in our minds.
We're caught forever on their battlelines:
Korea, Vietnam – we're never getting out.

And so the ballad's grief will never end:
. . . *Half-ovre, half ovre to Aberdour* . . .
I touched a wavecap with a flashing oar
And then went down before the rising wind.

MARILYN HACKER
TAKING LEAVE OF ZENKA

Rain slants down, crossing out the afternoon;
the roofs slick up, dry out, with cups of tea.
The telephone's adroit cacophony
interrupts what hasn't been begun
and what, again, won't be begun. Connection
to the next scene of a small tragedy.
(*Le Monde*'s been in the kiosks since half-past three
working up steam for next Sunday's election.)
In London, Zenka, who is eighty-four,

has colon cancer, and is going to die.
Spilled out, the intellectual champagne
her daily conversation used to pour.
Immobile, she awaits hot soup or pain
or large-print explanations in the sky.

The large-print explanations in the sky
are merely clouds, and what they spell is weather.
The wind re-sets them; they disperse, or gather
and loose their contents on the passers-by.
Tiepolo blue bannered behind the grey
edges diminishing to cotton and feather
mean shower and sunset might occur together
later, this mutable afternoon in May.
The women on the geriatric ward
were mostly not too certain where they were.
One, whose high-cheekboned face had made me stop,
soothed, in that place, by its austere accord,
vomited blankly into her lap
while no one turned around to look at her.

While no one turned around to look at her,
Zenka entranced with wit, mordant and dry,
uncompromising in its scrutiny
of foibles. One could easily incur
a sentence like a briskly shutting door –
but it would open on hilarity
over a lunch of what she'd call a pie
(quiche from Leclerc) and salad; a murmur
of breeze and meridional midday exchange
beyond the terrace. Tough as the transplants
– azaleas and hibiscus – in her garden,
she found the world peculiar, but not strange,
with little she'd condone, and much she'd pardon –
a British Jew who lived in southern France.

A British Jew who lived in southern France
had more than enough history to think
about, lunch dishes piled up in the sink,
her bookshelves groaning, and her common sense
(the roof's been fixed; the dog's been fed; the rent's
not due yet) keeping viable the link
between adventure (eloped – on the brink

of sixty!) and the day-by-daily chance-
taking routine. July, '78: I met
the vivid pair in the ceramics shop
which earned their slender living in Tourrettes-
sur-Loup, on an olive-terraced hilltop.
Tribal (though not initiated yet),
the slightest hint was all I had to drop.

The slightest hint was all I had to drop
to be acknowledged in the family
and hear its gossip: the *salon de thé*
up on the square two "girls" had opened up –
Tourrettes, to hear them, was a *gîte d'étape*
for "ours": the clerk in the *épicerie*,
the gallery, the jewelers . . . Were Marie
and I a couple? Was not asked. I stopped
by the next day, and chose an inkwell, glazed
in opalescent slate, for my singular
friend, who was ill, who is wholly without pair.
We were invited to come back and eat
with them the next evening: such a discreet
acceptance, I accepted, not amazed.

Acceptance I accepted, not amazed
(I was that young) to think that numinous
landscapes, miraculous acquaintances
were in the world for me to seize and praise
(in sentences fortuitously phrased).
But if I could adopt my ancestors,
it was because Zenka invented hers:
conceived, accomplished, rehearsed and raised
herself, not losing sight of the East End.
Self-rescued, she became a rescuer
from small ads and suburban oligarchs,
monoglot minds, despotic matriarchs.
Expatriate, she brought the wit to cure
a boyish woman soldier of her wound.

The boyish woman soldier, with a wound
deep now as earth in which a life's interred
shed avian grace, mercurial black bird
on multinational mourners around
the grave, around the *hors d'oeuvres* where they thronged, beyond

the sliding window to the garden. Blurred
in June fog, suburban yellow roses, shirred
peach, bloom where they were planted by her friend.
Slow, but a gentleman in grey, her son,
stumping his crutch, a question, on the floor,
teaches himself absence's rudiments:
"Zenka, in the kitchen, make tea, no more",
Below the Channel, trains tunnel to France.
Rain slants down, crossing out the afternoon.

ANTHONY HECHT
WITNESS

Against the enormous rocks of a rough coast
The ocean rams itself in pitched assault
And spastic rage to which there is no halt;
Foam-white brigades collapse; but the huge host

Has infinite reserves; at each attack
The impassive cliffs look down in gray disdain
At scenes of sacrifice, unrelieved pain,
Figured in froth, aquamarine and black.

Something in the blood-chemistry of life,
Unspeakable, impressive, undeterred,
Expresses itself without needing a word
In this sea-crazed Empedoclean Strife.

It is a scene of unmatched melancholy,
Weather of misery, cloud-cover of distress,
To which there are no witnesses, unless
One counts the briny, tough and thorned sea-holly.

MARK HALLIDAY
AUTUMN COMMUNION

October is a wave washing shadows over the future,
and the light dashes sideways like a dreaming pony.
I think of Vallejo coughing in the alleys of Madrid.
To not be appreciated is very bad. The wind curls
and I think of Baudelaire's rogue swan
and I move to the kitchen to hear what Gwen is saying
about raking the leaves in time for municipal pickup.
October is a dream in the mind of a yellow-and-red marble
shot by a boy who has disappeared among the sycamores,
and I think of Neruda tossing his cap from a balcony
and the way time winds its hair into a bun of regret.
I descend upon the sofa with my toast.
It tastes like a bun of regret, a grace of ash.
I think of those who have lost what can never
be found . . . It is something without a name,
made of silence and light, time, and an ounce of tears.
Gwen says she wants the leaves raked before we touch
the Sunday *Times*. I think of
three poets with mustaches who are thinking of
Lorca or Edward Hopper or Rimbaud or Crane
and I gaze, gaze, gaze out the window upon leaves
that fall so gently yet swiftly upon the humbled grass.
I think of Vallejo – no, wait, I already thought of Vallejo
– I think of Cezanne who may have been a cousin of
my great-grandmother on my mother's side – ah, the ripple
of linkage, the nameless oneness, and the swift tumble
of the hands of the tossing trees. *Whack* says the screen door
for Gwen has left the house, and I think of Mandelstam
and how in a way he thought I'm sure of me.

FRED VOSS
25 VENDING MACHINE
CANDY BARS TO CHOOSE FROM

Why do we not live naked in caves in harmony with the universe
like all the other animals?
Is it to stand at a bank teller window at 9 a.m.?
Is it to have walls between each other,
to drive to a factory 10,000 times in a life without really
knowing why
to watch an apple fall
and think of gravity
or wind a watch on an airplane
or crush a man's hand
to gain a confession
or build the tallest monument on earth to yourself
or blow up a mountain
or fill a sea with filth
or strike terror into millions of hearts with a word,
why
are we the only animals on earth to put on clothes
and build sewer systems and think
of things to do?
Is it to count the days
and take photographs of each other
and try to beat each other to the ribbon in 100-yard dashes?
Is it to invent the can opener
or stand on a corner with your hand out hungry and have
thousands of cars pass you by?
Is it to hang like a fly in a spiderweb watching death creep
closer and closer in a retirement home?
Is it to pull the wings off a butterfly
or know how the valves in the heart work
or is it to listen
to the ninth symphony of Beethoven
or stand before the Pieta of Michelangelo
or lie in the grass and read Walt Whitman,
trying to recapture a little bit of all
we have lost?

Out of Neverland

JOHN GREENING ON THE LOST BOYS OF AMERICAN POETRY

WHAT DECIDES WHETHER a particular American poet finds any readers over here? It would be good to think that it was more than the whim of publishers, who choose Lynch because he's an undertaker, Doty because he writes about Aids, Olds because she writes about sex, or Kleinzahler because he does what we expect from an American poet – and even includes the word "whisky" in his title. All fine writers, but the fact is that what we regard here as mainstream US verse ain't necessarily so. Indeed, there are several popular poets on the shelves of small-town American bookstores who are barely known over here – John Ciardi, Maxine Kumin, Wendell Berry... Some we once knew and have forgotten, others we have never had the chance even to forget.

Why some of these names have been consigned to Neverland is understandable. Take Carl Sandburg (1878-1967), for instance – still muscling in on those shelves alongside Frost and Ginsberg, still a poet of considerable popular appeal: rooted in Whitman and the Civil War, blossoming as a 'sixties free spirit, folk-songs and all. He is generally ignored in Britain not because his work has been unavailable, but because – for all his gestures of universality – time has shown him to be essentially a provincial poet. And just as Betjeman is unlikely to go down well in Chicago, so Chicago's own chronicler never really lifts us out from between the sky-scrapers. There is the appearance of precision in the imagery, but it is really a mist; and the sound of the verse is unrelievedly flat. Sandburg's poetry will only "work" if one brings to it some appropriate emotions – the requisite love of the Midwest, of America and its history.

The same cannot be said of Archibald MacLeish, however, who was born fourteen years after Sandburg, and lived through to 1982. But they were both very public figures for much of their lives, each playing the part of Grand Old Man, involving themselves in and writing about politics and public affairs. The difference was that Sandburg's easy-going Captain-Hook-in-Levis style matched perfectly the mood of the sixties, whereas most of MacLeish's followers (those who could stomach his becoming a war-time propagandist and Assistant Secretary of State) aged and died with him. In fact, one of Sandburg's most original and musical poems

was dedicated to MacLeish after the latter had been summoned before Congress to "divulge the portents and meanings of his poems":

> Nobody noogers the shaff of a sloo.
> Nobody slimbers a wench with a winch
> Nor higgles armed each with a niggle
>   and each the flimdrat of a smee
>   each the inbiddy hum of a smoo (...)
>   ('On a Flimmering Floom You Shall Ride')

The nonsense lyric is, I suppose, the consummation of mistiness. There is not much humour (or much rhythm) elsewhere in the 676 pages of Sandburg's *Complete* [no nonsense] *Poems*!

But in MacLeish's similarly vasty *Collected* there is a remarkable variety of styles. A welcome contrast, and clearly a much more interesting poet to British readers, yet it is perhaps this very versatility – together with our national distaste for smiling public poets – which has led to his neglect. His name got lost in the mess of definitions in mid-century, when European readers wanted to know whether their American poets were like Frost or Williams or Stevens: Archibald MacLeish is like all and none of them. Ironically, he is best known for his famous definition of poetry in 'Ars Poetica': "A poem should not mean / But be". What makes his poems "be" is the force and character of the voice, whatever style it has adopted. After reading Sandburg, it is like having crossed the Great Plains to emerge in a landscape of lush word music: "My heart, have we not heard / The birds at Avignon and in the roofs / of Arles cool doves?" He is as mellifluous as Stevens without his obscurity or silliness (see 'Selene Afterwards'). Elsewhere he can be as "grave and level" as Frost, be poignantly imagistic with the Poundians, or yoke Masefield to the Metaphysicals in his much-anthologised 'You, Andrew Marvell' (whose title is that poem's only baffling element – unless we are supposed to remember the sun being made to run at the end of 'To His Coy Mistress'). Recognisable traits are an anguished, emphatic or ornamental repetition (as in the sonnet 'The End of the World', perhaps his most striking poem of all) and an invigorating, unpedantic use of full rhyme. The *Collected* is rich in surprises: a Shakespearean pastiche, a long poem on Einstein, jazz-influenced lyrics, plenty of satire, and always an exciting tension between the private and public voices. A good *Selected* for the English market would make all this clear and is long overdue.

Reputations come and go, of course, often in response to the social climate. For years we were persuaded that Robert Lowell was the next American genius after Eliot. A tortured religious New England male was just the ticket – even when *Notebook* appeared and reappeared as *History*, even when he started to recycle other people's letters into his own poems. Now Lowell seems to have disappeared – and, lo! Elizabeth Bishop is in his place. Perhaps she in turn will vanish to reveal Marianne Moore – like some archetypal Mrs Darling to her Wendy – as the true mother of modern American poets. Whatever, there is certainly a new willingness to rescue women poets (Amy Clampitt, for instance) from oblivion, even if mid-century figures like Edna St Vincent Millay, H.D. and Louise Bogan are left floundering in the footnotes, and certain contemporaries (Rachel Hadas, Debora Greger, Emily Grosholz) have yet to find their niche. American women writers are at last beginning to get a fair hearing in Britain. And some would argue that their opportunities have too long been blocked by well-known white males like Theodore Roethke (1908-1963), the next poet I want to highlight: Faber's 1968 *Collected* and 1969 *Selected* did indeed bring him a degree of popular acclaim here, and he had already had PBS successes. But with Roethke we have the problem of the wrong kind of recognition. Rather as we used to with Frost, we tend to think of him as a somewhat slight pastoral poet fit for school-anthologies. What we forget is that for many Americans (and for at least one Nobel Prize-winning Irishman) he was potentially the very greatest. In 1948, with *The Lost Son* he not only made possible the Confessional style (which many women poets have since found congenial), but as that endangered Confessionalist W. D. Snodgrass put it: "Roethke more than any other poet of his generation was offered the chance of true great-

> With Roethke we have the problem of the wrong kind of recognition... We tend to think of him as a somewhat slight pastoral poet fit for school-anthologies. What we forget is that for many Americans (and for at least one Nobel Prize-winning Irishman) he was potentially the very greatest.

ness... He was offered a virtual continent of language and fled from it...into the voice of Yeats". As with MacLeish, sheer versatility has worked against him, but so has his originality. Roethke may have chosen to adopt the masks of earlier masters, but behind them he remains one of the most extraordinary voices, one that can be heard (though it is seldom acknowledged) in the work of subsequent poets – not only the obvious ones like Plath, but others who have never crossed the Atlantic. Once we begin to hear Roethke's sweet madrigals behind the massed-bands and tickertape of Ashbery and O'Hara and Ginsberg, we can follow him into another America:

I dream of journeys repeatedly:
Of flying like a bat deep into a
    narrowing tunnel,
Of driving alone, without luggage,
    out a long peninsula,
The road lined with snow-laden
    second growth,
A fine dry snow ticking the wind
    shield,
Alternate snow and sleet, no on-
    coming traffic,
And no lights behind, in the blurred
    side-mirror,
The road changing from glazed tarface to a rubble of
    stone,
Ending at last in a hopeless sand-rut,
Where the car stalls,
Churning in a snowdrift
Until the headlights darken.

           (from 'The Far Field')

Roethke was no escapist. He could *not* escape: that was his tragedy. Snodgrass makes of him a Peter Pan who "in some desperate way never grew up", but 'The Far Field' shows that he was making his own painful way, not just trying to fly in the slipstream of Yeats or the Elizabethans.

Roethke's friendship with Stanley Kunitz (evident from his fascinating *Selected Letters*) was clearly a life-line to him. Kunitz remembers they "used to challenge each other to guess the dates of the most obscure poems we could find... We became so expert at the game that we almost never missed by more than ten years". The games stopped when Roethke died in a swimming accident in 1963 (the year of Sylvia Plath's death). Stanley Kunitz went on growing up – he was born three years before his friend – and is still around in his nineties; yet although there have been Kunitz books from British publishers, including a handsome 1979 selection from Seeker, and now Norton's *Passing Through: the Later Poems*, it can hardly be said that he is considered a major figure. He is inconvenient, not easy to fit into the available slots, a shape-shifter – his work develops from the very formal to the deceptively laid-back, hinging on the 1971 collection *The Testing-Tree*, which is where this latest 'New and Selected' begins. The very first poem 'Journal for my Daughter' includes a brief portrait of Roethke:

There was a big, blond uncle-bear,
wounded, smoke-eyed, wild,
who shambled from the west
with his bags full of havoc.
He spoke the bears' grunt-language,
waving his paws
and rocking on his legs ...

But this is a collection that is more than merely affectionately nostalgic: some of the work written in the last twenty years is outstanding: a version of the myth of Orpheus and Eurydice that rivals Rilke's, a long lament for a whale beached at Cape Cod, meditations on Protean themes of magic and transformation, and brief lyrics that are "lucid, innocent and true" – his own description of the kind of poetry he admires:

Great events are about to happen.
I have seen migratory birds
in unprecedented numbers
descend on the coastal plain,
picking the margins clean.
My bones are a family in their tent
huddled over a small fire
waiting for the uncertain signal
to resume the long march.

('Day of Foreboding')

Do we forget to read Kunitz just because he has not made his life sound interesting enough for us? Where are those breakdowns and bust-ups and binges? He is perceived as an academic poet: an editor, translator, reviewer. At the same time, he has not become associated with a particular movement or produced a standard text to keep his name in circulation the way, say, John Crowe Ransom

did. Or achieved a blockbuster novel as Robert Penn Warren did. Or edited an influential Penguin as Donald Hall did. He is often found in the index of another poet's letters (Bishop's *One Art*, for instance), less often in the contents pages of a contemporary anthology (e.g. Vendler's). If the name Kunitz does ring a bell, it is only the tinker-bell of criticism: as a critic he is in the superleague with Randall Jarrell, and no one should miss *A Kind of Order, a Kind of Folly*, which includes some of the best material we have on Roethke. As a translator he is tucked behind the names of Akhmatova or Mandelstam or Yevtushenko. Perhaps one day Stanley Kunitz will come to be acknowledged as the central figure that he is, discreetly influential on a whole range of poets familiar and unfamiliar. The other day, for example, I chanced upon an excellent 1996 volume by David Ignatow – one of those names frequently on American shelves, but whom I had never read – aptly titled *I Have a Name*, and it soon became apparent that he has been one of Kunitz's closest friends and dedicates a poem to him. I have no doubt that the same is true of a number of younger poets. We should not have to wait until Stanley Kunitz dies to realise his importance: try and get hold of this new selection.

Hayden Carruth (b.1921) is another poet who has sacrificed himself to the ticking crocodile of academia but is probably unknown here more because of his own reticence than for any other reason. He has not even had Kunitz's chances, and you will have to work hard to find a copy of his *Selected Poetry* (Collier Macmillan, 1985), but he clearly likes us, is haunted by us, by meadows and trees that evoke the Old rather than the New England he so often writes about:

The peace of green summer lay over this meadow so
                              deeply once
that I thought of England, cows lazy on the sward,
                              the great elm
rising above them in diaphanous arches, the meadow
                    that Marvell might have seen
from his study window but that I have never seen,
                                        yet I saw it
here. It *was* here, but that so long ago. And now the
                                              elms
of this region have mostly died, it is mid-November,
                              the gray season,
purple on wooded hills, the meadow is gray and
                              bare, the cows
are in their barn. I thought of England because so

many things I love
have come from England, many images in my
memory, although
I have never been there and have little hope that I
will ever go...
('Once and Again')

It is an American's privilege to write about England in that way, impossible to us now. One of the pleasures of Carruth's work is feeling him wear his heart on his sleeve so convincingly. Of course, it will be said that it is all too cosy, that Robert Frost is playing Nana to this particular Lost Boy. But he is no less respectable a model than Stevens or Williams, whatever fashion decrees; and while critics and publishers over here are still inclined to regard Frost as a destructive influence, he will go on performing his secret ministry long after the latest season's plums are eaten. Hayden Carruth's subjects are quietly autobiographical, essentially pastoral and domestic – life with his wife and son and the local "characters" of northern Vermont: most memorably Marshall Washer, who leaves the poet wondering "How can I learn the things / that are not transmissible? Marshall knows them. / He possesses them, the remnant of human worth / to admire in this world and I think to envy". But we are always conscious of a threat, both ecological ("the rural/slums par excellence that were your farms") and psychological. The possibility of

mental collapse has always been present, more obviously in his early work, *The Bloomingdale Papers*; and his later pastoral dramatic monologues and meditative eclogues are only keeping chaos just at arm's length – "black shapes / settle and shift and rise and settle again, talking / in the spruces". While a major sequence like 'Paragraphs' seems to have been sculpted from the very stuff of chaos itself, reclaiming the collage techniques of Modernism to explore deeper into territory Modernists would have derided. "A momentary stay against confusion" was Frost's definition of poetry, and it clarifies what we feel reading Hayden Carruth. As is the way with even mediocre American poets, he has been showered with awards and honours – including, to end where we began, the Carl Sandburg Prize. Perhaps our publishers will wake up to him now there's whisky in his title (*Scrambled Eggs and Whisky*, Copper Canyon, 1996)! But someone really ought to institute a prize for Poet Most Neglected in the United Kingdom. Additional contenders would be Ted Kooser, out on the Great Plains, who – according to Dana Gioia – "has written more perfect poems than any poet of his generation"; John Haines, up in Anchorage, who has devoted his life to tracking and capturing the spirit of Alaska; Peter Kane Dufault, waiting for the spark from heaven deep in the forests of upstate New York... Sometimes it does feel as though we little darlings never left the nursery.

Angels Away

By Dennis O'Driscoll

The Best American Poetry 1997
Edited by James Tate
Simon & Schuster, £20 hbk
ISBN 0 684 81454 4
£8.99 pbk
ISBN 0 684 81452 8

DIVIDING AMERICA'S PUBLISHED poets into camps – cooked and raw, neat and beat – is a largely redundant activity by now. One is tempted, cynically perhaps, to classify all of them as realists, albeit realists of a peculiarly modern kind. They are more likely to be found drafting applications for tenure-track teaching posts than drawing up manifestoes. If they experience Bohemia, it is as a country – visited on a grant or fellowship – from whose bourn the traveller returns with a clutch of quaint poems, ideal ballast for his or her next blurb-encrusted, award-bestrewn collection.

Far from being the unworldly loners of the popular image, poets strut through American campuses with titles of the "Distinguished Visiting Professor" type, which bespeak a poorly-developed sense of irony, self-mockery or hubris. Substantial incomes can be topped up – where alimony or social mobility requires – by positions as "core faculty" at Summer Writing Programs in off-season skiing towns. On the picturesque farms which serve as the private retreats of the more affluent, tie-beam barns will have been converted into studio space decorated with Navajo wall-hangings. There, the high productivity required to maintain high visibility in the little world of poetry is word-processed into existence – loose, runny slabs of narrative verse or tight, costive, self-conscious formal verse.

Poetry can take root anywhere and there are some poets who flourish in a university environment. Charles Wright, one of the most impressive contributors to *The Best American Poetry 1997* (his long poem, 'Disjecta Membra', seems poised between Li Po and Pound), is a university professor who described himself in his *Paris Review* interview as "almost a 100 percent product of the writing workshop system", adding that "it was not only good for me, but necessary as well". Although Wright serves as conclusive proof that workshops can work, he too has reservations about the current graduate programs, likening them to "feedlots or holding pens". Some of the most vibrant poetry in English is being written by teachers of creative writing; yet the notion of poetry originating almost exclusively in a university environment is no more palatable – and no less dangerous – than the over-dependency of farmers on one or two strains of high-yield wheat for the grain harvests of the Great Plains. It would be a disaster for poetry if its weedier cousins – rap and slam – were to be the only organic alternatives to the workshopped crop.

While the teaching of poetry is now an activity capable of providing secure employment and a career structure for many of America's poets, the poets themselves are not altogether happy. One thinks of Stevie Smith's pug:

O Pug, obstinate old nervous breakdown,
In the midst of *so* much love,
And such comfort,
Still to feel unsafe and be afraid . . .

Their unhappiness stems from the fact that the audience for their books (sumptuous two-tone hardbacks with tooled initials like family Bibles) is mainly limited to the enclosed orders of university poets, and students intent on picking up the tricks of the trade. They see themselves not as denizens of academia but as denim-clad free spirits; their dream is to be read and revered rather than hired to indulge the callow verse confessions of fledgling talents.

Introducing the latest *Forward* anthology (the *Best American* and *Forward* volumes – both compiled from a year's poetry publications – are transatlantic kin), John Fuller sagely remarked: "Most poetry eventually joins the vast shelves of the unread and most readers of poetry follow a beaten track. Time, which is said to be the mother of truth, can all too easily confirm habit and lay its slow dust on the unclamorous". "Time" will have to work overtime to sift through the vast rubble of late twentieth-century American poetry, to see how much remains that is living, breathing and deserving of rescue. "Unclamorousness", however, is not an accusation one would level against the more horn-tooting contributors to *The Best American Poetry 1997*, guest-edited by James Tate (who supplies a first-rate introduction). As you struggle through the triumphal commentaries of the poets on their own poems (published at the back of the book like answers to brain-teasers), you begin to feel glad to be facing these authors across a page rather than from the front row of a poetry reading.

Though his search for balance can sometimes lead to blandness, David Lehman's informative and elegant forewords, as series editor, are one of the reasons I look forward to each year's *Best American Poetry* volume. Lehman's essays are a kind of State of the Poetry Union address and have appeared since the anthology was inaugurated in 1988. Also generally useful (and something which the *Forward* anthologies should emulate) are the detailed notes on contributors which are included. These are a boon if you want to track down further work by the poets in the anthology who really *are* the "best" – poets of the calibre of Robert Hass ('Interrupted Meditation' is the anthology's masterpiece), Albert Goldbarth and Billy Collins – as well as less-established writers like Catherine Bowman and Beth Lisick whose lively prose-poems make you wonder whether their other work is equally enjoyable. Unfortunately, Catherine Bowman is one of the poets whose patience-fraying explanatory note at the back of the book tempts you to reconsider your favourable judgement of her poem at the front ("I'll start out by saying that I do not believe that all of society is murderous..."); Lisick, on the other hand, is witty and snappy, summarising her poem in a single shimmering sentence which stifles one's unworthy bias against her membership of a poetry slam team, performing in places like the Lollapalooza Festival: "It was written for parents who retire to gated communities of steel-framed homes and former television stars who drink nightcaps in their pajamas while gardenias bloom in the desert".

Given the earnestness and self-importance of so many of the contributors to this anthology, both the MFA Boomers and their elders ("When I gave him the poem, he said, 'I wasn't expecting anything this good'", goes one double-edged example), I began to wonder if the poetry slammers might not be needed, after all, to challenge the complacencies of the contemporary academy, just as the Beat poets – for all their superficiality – famously did in the Fifties. One minor task I have in mind for the slammers is to shoo away some of the angels, who are so common in American writing as to have become the pigeons of the poetry world. Intended to automatically bestow spirituality and significance, mystery and profundity on poems, they represent one of the nervous flutters of millennial verse. In *The Best American Poetry 1997* alone, you will find at least eight poems (one or two, admittedly, quite good) in which angels make a flying visit or fall to earth for a refuelling stop. It is high time their wings were clipped.

STEPHEN DOBYNS
THE APPRECIATION OF BEAUTY

Prime Mover took a breather to admire the view:
sunrise in the valley made green grass glitter.
Belly full of breakfast, Prime Mover expressed wind:
hot gases, minuscule particles rushed outward.

Tell me, is a day equally long for fruit fly
and tiger? Within one universe, can't a cluster
of atoms enclose another? Amidst swirling methane
at least one particle contained a flicker of life.

Jiffies in one world, millenniums in another.
The presence of water, the presence of light:
soon fire was discovered, then the wheel.
Prime Mover sighed, rubbed his belly, strolled on.

Science and religion intertwined when on one speck
a white-coated upstart articulated the Big Bang.

THE SONNET HISTORY

JOHN WHITWORTH
AMERICAN PIE (DUET FOR TWO VOICES)

Bass: I'm rough and tough. I smoke and drink and swear.
           To hell with European airs and graces,
           I'm wild and woolly as a grizzly bear.
           I write Free Verse, untamed and in my braces.

Sop: I call on Fame who never called on me.
           I keep my language, like my body, chaste.
           I write a thousand poems, publish three.
           My Art is perfect though my Life is waste.

Duet: We are the People, following the sun,
           We are the Gods, electric with creating,
           The Brooklyn bounder and the Amherst nun,
           New ways of seeing, being, punctuating.
           We are the stars of hope, the stripes of sorrow.
           We are America. We are Tomorrow.

Historical Sicknotes

by Sean O'Brien

JOHN ASHBERY

Wakefulness

Carcanet, £6.95
ISBN 1 857 54334 3

The Mooring of Starting Out: the First Five Books of Poetry

Carcanet, hbk, £25
ISBN 1 857 54366 1

WAKEFULNESS IS THE septuagenarian John Ashbery's seventeenth collection of poems. Given the tooth-grinding torpor much of it induces, the title (changed in the proofs from *The Whispering Gallery*) seems like a hostage to fortune. To mix metaphors like Ashbery, much of the book is a desert of local, wilful ingenuity across which the poet can be heard nattering on and habitually juxtaposing until the reader finds himself abandoning equipment – rifle, boots, water-bottle – and running for the horizon as delirium sets in. After a very long time, though, 'One Man's Poem' appears like an oasis:

> The waves of freshman and sophomore grief
> slide by me somehow.
> We are old and dated
> and cannot of our lives make any sense.

The stanza bears out in the baldest fashion a remark Ashbery made in an interview in this magazine in 1985 (Volume 75, Number 1): "For a long time it seemed to me as though my poetry didn't have a subject in the way that poetry is supposed to, but...getting older is a thing I've been writing about all the time". Whether the lines quoted here have an autobiographical force is irrelevant – something Ashbery insists on elsewhere in the interview. In their plainness they are clearly felt. It is interesting that the inversion in the last line quoted seems to nod back at Stevens, the American poet to whom Ashbery is reputedly most indebted (and from whose marmoreal utterances he has worked so hard to separate himself).

Getting older is one thing, yet the idea of having a historical perspective, something more than a personal experience of time, seems almost foreign to Ashbery's work. In the words of a fine earlier time-poem, 'Soonest Mended', it has always lived perceptually hand to mouth "on the margins of society". While Ashbery's poems often talk of how things used to be, and how they changed, and have arguably made a style from the way the change continues under the gaze of the poem and in turn affects that gaze – see the touching 'Mixed Feelings' from *Self-Portrait in a Convex Mirror* – there is rarely any ordinary human sense of having begun somewhere in particular and being likely to end up somewhere else, too. This is a condition of the instability of identity which has been spoken of as one of his concerns, but in the the latest book it comes with a lack of the dialectical friction which could make the flow of things dramatically compelling for the reader whose sense of the world is not the same as the poet's. Colin Falck makes the astute observation that in Ashbery's verse "there are poetic images to be found, but they float in and out of the writing – mentioned, as philosophers might say – rather than used...and are never allowed any fictional time and space in which to develop their potential significances". How could they be? Ashbery's enormous, minutely detailed energy everywhere acknowledges itself as being at the mercy of process; he seeks to make a virtue of this predicament, a strength from an historical sicknote. The melancholy which partly arises from this has given his work a powerful part of its grace, for instance in one of his finest earlier poems, the brief 'Summer' from *The Double Dream of Spring* (1970), though here Ashbery stands in a closer relationship than usual to a lyric poetry such as Rilke's:

> ...and winter, the twitter
> Of cold stars at the pane, that describes with broad
> gestures
> This state of being that is not so big after all.
> Summer involves going down a steep flight of steps
>
> To a narrow ledge over the water. Is this it, then,
> This iron comfort, these reasonable taboos,
> Or did you mean it when you stopped? And the face
> Resembles yours, the one reflected in the water.

There is an Audenesque dimension here, too, in those "reasonable taboos". When Ashbery acknowledges the idea of "making" as distinct from simply uttering, he becomes memorable. Perhaps it will in time be thought that he suffers a kind of literalism more usually associated with the "raw", democratic, inclusive strain in American poetry, that of Whitman and Williams, rather than the self-conscious aestheticism of Stevens. In the *Poetry Review* interview he seemed to declare as much:

> What people say to each other when they are trying very hard to communicate is always sloppy and unsatisfying and full of uncompleted sentences and thought. Nevertheless, this is the trope that we all use when we are trying to make ourselves understood, and I'm sure there must be a good reason for this or the situation wouldn't have evolved like that. It's that kind of speech I find very poignant and moving. We all know Mallarmé's dictum about purifying the language of the tribe. In my case I don't feel it needs purifying. I try to encourage it.

Of course, few people would really care to be judged by seemingly off-the-cuff comments like this, but Ashbery's "argument" is unsatisfactory. It tries to make a partial truth the whole of the matter – for, on the contrary, people do sometimes express themselves very clearly in times of need; while the language of a poem does not simply incorporate, still less simply consist of, the language of life: it selects, and – however simply – it shapes. The problem with *Wakefulness* is that the shaping is perfunctory. The very range of possible referents, tones, registers, disruptions, juxtapositions, non-sequiturs, moments of lyric clarity, happy accidents and bits of mischief has also made the work by turns irritating, depressing and – at times – boring. Almost as if aware of this, in 'More About Getting into School', the poet asks, "Is nothing uninteresting any more?". Ashbery for the most part ignores his admirable gift for exploiting the contrast between disparate or peculiar materials and assured, elegant, extensive sentences, something he has possessed since 'The Instruction Manual' in his first book *Some Trees* (1956). Instead, there are little

catalogues of perceptual dissonance. He has in some sense "moved on", but the effect is of monotony in variety. It's hardly fair to excerpt from a book that reads like a continuum of white noise, but see 'The Spacious Firmament':

> A great equator did him in, in the fullness of time
> waited at the end of my hall, cobbled quodlibets,
> procession towards a context. Capitalist
> proceedings forced it into a runoff.
> Model villages provide all sorts of
> plumbing. Cherry blossoms cascade
>
> in spring, don't last long.
> I think we shall be moving to
> the dance baths on the river...

Liberation has become mannerism, poetry something written by the length. You could argue that the monotony is of a particularly American sort – teeming and "ungovernable", containing multitudes but strangely homogeneous – an imperial monotony which, in its Tiggerish energy, comes to seem somewhat oppressive. Life is strange, multiple, subject to instant revision, the poems suggest – but this has become an assumption rather than a stimulus, and the effect here is sometimes like what in primary school used to be called "copying out", or, come to think of it, as if the poet had been punished by being given lines. He has suffered for his art, and now it seems to be our turn. On the whole, as far as *Wakefulness* is concerned, I think I'll give it a miss, thanks. But it should go without saying that many contemporary poets whose preoccupations are apparently rather different from Ashbery's owe him (and Frank O'Hara and Kenneth Koch) a debt for suggesting some ways in which a curiosity about the medium of poetry itself, and about the workings of what used to be called the imagination, and about the relationship of "official" to "vulgar" culture, may all be accommodated in poetry. Carcanet are to be congratulated on producing a particularly beautiful and useful book in *The Mooring of Setting Out*, to which new readers are directed.

Heavyweight

E. A. MARKHAM ON AN ATTEMPT TO CANONIZE THE AFRICAN-AMERICAN EXPERIENCE

The Norton Anthology: African-American Literature

General eds. Henry Louis Gates, Jr. and Nellie Y. McKay
Norton, £21
ISBN 0 398 95908 2

THIS IS BIG book. Heavy book. And the post office damage it, you know. Like they don't like black people to have book so big and heavy. I did go to the shop and ask to weigh it; and everyone impress. But enough of black talk. Non-black people do it so much better these days.

So how does one approach a literary institution like Norton? It's different from a Penguin which comes in the sort of size that doesn't intimidate the reader. Of course Norton is a resource, not of literary archeology, exactly, as the volumes get updated; and one that looks splendid on the shelf.

This book has been, we're told in the preface, ten years in the making, involving, as well as the general editors, nine "period" editors (who had autonomy over their selection of material) and scores of advisors spread across the nation's universities. Gates, himself, is at Harvard and McKay at the university of Wisconsin, Madison. So this is as canonical as a book comprising 2,665 pages can get. So why does the very fact of this volume raise the old anxieties that its subject is being marginalized?

The editors justify the project by reminding us of the importance placed on imaginative writing (as well as on mathematical calculation) by writers and thinkers of the European Enlightenment of the 18th century. By not writing down their narratives and poetry, Africans (who were deemed not to have access to such things) were ruled to be lacking in humanity, and hence susceptable to being enslaved. The philosopher David Hume was very keen on this idea. This, what we might call, slave mentality on the part of the beacons of the "Enlightenment" was adopted by the victims, initially, perhaps, as a form of self-protection, then internalized and, like a germ (not a gene) found to be stubbornly resistant. In this bleak drama enter Phillis Wheatley (1753?-1784) signalling hope.

The first black person to publish a book of poetry in English[1] Wheatley was subject to a test, a sort of viva at a courthouse in Boston in 1773 to see whether plagiarism could be detected – figures from Greek and Latin myth and literature adorn the work, which tends towards the heroic couplet, in the manner of Pope. The panel, eighteen good men and true, including the governor of the colony, took the (perhaps) eighteen-year-old slave through her paces before signing the "attestation" that the work was, indeed, Wheatley's.

There is sometimes the temptation, provoked again by some of the middle sections of this fine book, to protest that African American literature oppresses the reader with its grand themes of slavery/rebellion; racial prejudice/civil rights; the African idyll/American nightmare. True. But the literature is informed by a collective sense of the determined and often bizarre hurdles (removed now in haste and, perhaps, panic) to its realization. The book reminds us of one such example: a few decades before Wheatley, after a slave rebellion in South Carolina in 1739, laws were brought in "making two forms of African literacy: mastery of letters and mastery of the drum" a punishable offence.

So, to the book: turning to an area I know reasonably well, The Harlem Renaissance, I register little surprise. Du Bois isn't there with the other residents – McKay, Hurston, Garvey, Langston Hughes, etc. – but he's in the section before, so I'm reduced to quibbling that Eric Walrond is again represented by 'The Wharf Rats', a story recently featured in Viking's *Harlem Renaissance Reader* (1994) and in Penguin's *Book of Caribbean Short Stories* (1996): one wonders whether some of the complete, easily-accessible texts included elsewhere in the volume (Lorraine Hansberry's 61-page *A Raising in the Sun*, for example) mightn't be extracted to give broader representation to the work of earlier figures consigned to "anthology" pieces – too much autonomy by the period editors? But then, room is made here for the complete text of *Cane*, Jean Toomer's 1923 masterwork of sketches,

---

[1] *Poems on Various Subjects, Religious and Moral By Phillis Wheatley, Negro Servant to Mr. John Wheatley, of Boston, in New England.*

stories, poems & a novella invoking the world of
rural Georgia and the ghettos of Washington DC.
Its formal innovation still impresses, and its evoca-
tion of the South said to be suggestive of Faulkner's
– though the latter's first novel was published three
years after Cane.

The book is divided into seven sections: 'The
Vernacular Tradition'; 'The Literature of Slavery
and Freedom (1746-1865)' – Phillis Wheatley,
Olaudah Equiano, Sojourner Truth, Frederick
Douglas, etc.; 'Literature of the Reconstruction to
the New Negro Renaissance: 1865-1919'; 'The
Harlem Renaissance: 1919-1940'; 'Realism,
Naturalism, Modernism: 1940-1960'; 'The Black
Arts Movement: 1960-1970' and, finally,
'Literature Since 1970'. In editing, strict
chronology is modified by a lightly drawn thematic
approach which works well for, maybe, four
sections, leaving the others thin in literature but
with some compensatory historical/political reso-
nance. 'The Black Arts Movement: 1960-1970'
comes off worst, perhaps, because of its obviousness
(it's all a Black Arts Movement, really) – and that's
despite Baraka (*Dutchman*) whose protest holds up.
Much that would make the movement literarily
adventurous is hived off – Baldwin and Kaufman
one way (Bob Kaufman was a poet who protested
againt American military involvement in Vietnam
through self-imposed silence), and the better bits of
M. L. King etc., another way, into the Vernacular
Tradition. (There is a feeling of disappointment,
now, revisiting Cleaver's *Soul On Ice*, Sonia
Sanchez, etc.)

Apart from the section labeled 'Realism,
Naturalism. Modernism: 1940-1960' which
includes substantial work by, among others,
Richard Wright, Ralph Ellison, Gwendolyn
Brooks, James Baldwin and Lorraine Hansberry,
the first and last sections are of especial interest.
The Vernacular ranges over time encompassing
spirituals, gospel, the blues, secular songs, jazz, rock,
sermons and folk tales. As well as rap.

What is so clearly reflected here, with what one
might call a "folk" tradition, is the opening up of
space within which the tradition could absorb influ-
ences from outside – and inform scribal work –
Ellison, Langston Hughes, Morrison, and, of
course, Mark Twain. The result of this melange, as
the world knows, is tonal, verbal and intellectual
sophistication: I'm thinking of the hope/consola-
tion tightrope of the blues; the wit/self-mockery
habit of secular songs ('Stakolee', etc.); the having-

fun-while-remembering-the-blues quality of
jazz/while creolizing its range of influences. I'm
thinking of the breadth of historical reference in the
sermons. King's 'I Have a Dream', in its context
(delivered to sanitation workers in Tennessee
pressing for higher wages and an end to maltreat-
ment by white supervisors – is the real context, not
that he was murdered next day), causes us to be
impressed by its structuring, its pacing, its aware-
ness of the existence of a world larger than America.

This takes me to the last section. The achieve-
ment is impressive. Here we have, in Toni Morrison
and August Wilson, the dramatist, two writers of
rare distinction, whose work – equal to the best of
Ellison and Wright – still rooted in the black
community, provokes a response more complex and
problematic than rage or guilt. We have, also, in
Jamaica Kincaid – now an American, not an
Antiguan citizen – someone approaching that
distinction, should Kincaid check the slide towards
lyricism. Allied to that are a host of literary stars –
Walker, Baraka, Shange, Angelou, Walter Mosley,
Rita Dove, all of whom have written fine books
(though Walker and Angelou should seriously steer
clear of poetry). We might also spare a thought for
the underhyped – a brother like Ishmael Reed (b.
1938) still going his random, anarchic way, issuing
strange manifestoes (shades of the Pataphysics of
Jarry?). There are many roads, now, to go down.

In the context of their history there are at least
three encouraging things about black writers in
America today. They are picking up the prizes –
Guggenheim and Rockefeller Fellowships.
National Endowment and Creative Arts Public
Service Grants as well as National Book Awards.
Prizes range from the Obie and Outer Critics Circle
(theatre) Awards through to the Pulitzer and the
Poet Laureateship (Rita Dove) to the Nobel (Toni
Morrison).

Also (this is the second thing) – this volume bears
it out to embarrassing effect – most of today's
writers featured here seem to be university profes-
sors, their literary preparation exemplary. Consider
Ntozake Shange's adolescent reading: Dostoevsky,
Melville, Carson McCullers, Edna St. Vincent
Millay, Simon de Beauvoir and Jean Genet. Many
of her colleagues would amend that merely to add
an interest in the classics – Black British writers
please note. Allied to this acquaintance with the
world's literature is the participation in a whole
range of art forms; an intellectual curiosity and an
interest in the Third World which might or might

not be Africa, heirs to truly renaissance figures like W. E. B. Du Bois (1868-1963) who renounced his American citizenship in the end.

So the authors can no longer claim exclusive ghetto involvement, or an unmediated condition of underprivilege (even being part of a nation state that is large, powerful, and dominating, helps rather than hinders a sense of belonging, and is of literary value even to members of the Nation of Islam). The result, overall, is encouraging. In poetry: Audre Lorde's multiple (feminist, lesbian) identities are hauntingly evoked; June Jordan breaks through, occasionally, into comedy, Shange's imitators now know that quirkiness, learning, wit and passion are expected of a young black woman writing about her life, and Rita Dove, in her 'Mother Love' sonnets raids the Demeter-Persephone myth-kitty for her American mother-daughter meditation. The final entry in the book is one Essex Hemphill (1957-1995) strongly playing the gay card. I was tempted to see this as hopeful, then I looked again at his dates. Inevitably, you're drawn to those left out: Elizabeth Alexander, for example. The lightness of touch and intellectual sophistication of her *The Venus Hottentot* (1990) suggest one future for black writing.

Who is this book for? (Let me pass on some statistics: there are 120 writers included, 52 of whom are women.) Also we might confirm that many writers here enjoy dual citizenship, both of the Black Republic and of the American Empire of Letters as represented by other Nortons[2]. The editors quote a *New York Times* report of 1996 that African Americans purchased 160 million books a year. (How do they know these things? And aren't people uneasy living in a society that knows these things?) But that is one possible outlet.

Though the Norton pitch is clearly for the "classroom market", with "generous selections of major figures": *Narrative of the Life of Frederick Douglass, An American Slave*, W. E. B. Du Bois' *The Souls Of Black Folk*, Morrison's *Sula*, August Wilson's *Fences*, among the complete texts. The editors also sought to produce a work "abundant enough to give the instructors choices...and annotation to free the student of the need to use reference books" (dodgy). The aim, too, was an anthology "comfortably portable, so students can carry it to class". Now, this anthology weighs 1,500 grammes. It heavy. So like they telling we something. We Americans are big, big people. And we strong.

[2] Morrison, unlike many of her African American contemporaries, doesn't appear in the *Norton Anthology of American Literature*, but this, surely, must be at her request.

RITA DOVE
SING SONG

When I was young, the moon spoke in riddles
and the stars rhymed. I was a new toy
waiting for my owner to pick me up.

When I was young. I ran the day to its knees.
There were trees to swing on, crickets for capture.

I was narrowly sweet, infinitely cruel,
tongued in honey and coddled in milk,
sunburned and silvery and scabbed like a colt.

And the world was already old.
And I was older than I am today.

THE CLASSIC POEM

AMERICAN NEOCLASSICISM. OF course we find something missing when we read Richard Wilbur. Leslie Feidler, one of the dimmer beacons of American LitCrit, complained that he found in Wilbur "no passion, no insanity". That was 1964, mind you, when insanity was a good career move. Nowadays we'd probably complain that he doesn't express indeterminacy.

One well behaved sentence – six epigrammatic lines addressed to a race of dead poets; one image – introduced in the only line to vary the metrical pattern. Wilbur likens the dead poets' single line to a trace erased when the page itself evaporates. Note: *page*, the blank snow field which, as I read back along the metaphor, becomes the purity of milk. The mother tongue (the vernacular Etruscan as opposed to the Latin father tongue) is a *matrix* [L., female animal used for breeding, – think of twins suckled by a wolf – same root as *mater,* but also, according to Webster's definitions "1) something within or from which something else originates, develops, or takes form" as a poem crystallises in that joining of world and mind or "3) a natural material in which something is embedded" as a sandal may be embedded in snow]. These are micrometer precisions.

But consider Webster's sixth definition: "6) a main clause that contains a subordinate clause", which describes the poem under discussion. Of course we find something missing when we read Richard Wilbur. It's missing from us, though, not him.

RICHARD WILBUR

TO THE ETRUSCAN POETS

Dream fluently, still brothers, who when young
Took with your mothers' milk the mother tongue,

In which pure matrix, joining world and mind,
You strove to leave some line of verse behind

Like a fresh track across a field of snow,
Not reckoning that all could melt and go.

Reprinted by permission of Faber and Faber from *Collected Poems*.

POETRY REVIEW

41

STEPHEN BURT
DERIVATIVE STYLES

Attractive woods we'd camped in; holiday
Villages like mirages; piers and shores
Dreamt of, then gladly seen and occupied;
Cities like chess, whose endgame midnight squares
We won on moves our teachers' teachers tried –
The best of us outgrew them. Others stayed,
Content with their companions, or unsure
Why we should want to "strike out on our own".

– "Become yourself". For most of us, who won't,
Derivative styles, old schools, and cracked codes give us
Subjects and habits, not to reassure,
But to converse with those who will outlive us:
Ungratefulness too high a price for power,
We chose being good; want, well, what others want;

Pace, ill, the trails we scanned from the screen doors
Of houses we grew up in; print reports
With diagrams of slight, or local, worth,
And overlook, or stint, the unexplored
Wide friendless open spaces to our South,
As if we thought old woods could yield new cures.

FLORENCE ELON
TWO-TONE

Solitude has a tone
at first – monotonous, hollow
middle C – and then
that pitch sustained by flute
until its player's breath
gives out.

Sometimes a second instrument
joins in,
doubling – not harmony –
the same note an octave lower
for a moment.
One ends. And one goes on

SANDRA McPHERSON
TOY SOLDIER

ca 1930

With the ethereal radio man,
his spinning wheel of fine wire,
and with the disheveled wounded,
who are legion, child, you play,
but your favorite is the warrior
whose hand is raised to smite
this gong with whatever
that musical utensil is called,
that weapon against gongs
that makes metal suffer
great shudders of urgent tone.
They swamp the jittery lull.
And see: As it would *not* be
in the symphony, the instrument
is shingled "Gas Alarm".

And when, child, you make
believe, the small gong swinging
in the current of your breath,
you imagine the performance,
whole round quavers ebbing,
and you know you should
envision the strangling mist.
But why, when you're safe?
The soldier hasn't struck it yet.
His mask's filtering eyes
match battered tin camp cups,
let him search the mud-green
blasted battle map, sigh in no
toxin. Toxin, tocsin,
you play with the names.

He is no toy Tchaikovsky,
but a child cannot know that yet.
The instant the alarmist's
duty becomes music,
it re-composes the world.
Except it save someone,
a whole symphony's
worth of men,
it sings without the slightest
resonance of the sublime.
Is there no sorrow with a toy?
Eventually there is,
but it may take year upon year
to reach that threshold
when the child amused
into manhood will volunteer.

JULIE O'CALLAGHAN
THINGS

My guy loves things –
and I'm a shop till you drop gal
so I better get it together.
Here's what one ad says:
"You'll wonder how we got her
into an uncut standard milk bottle –
a unique gift item – Cow in a Bottle – $25".
Oh man, that would be cool.
But, like, I bet he'd *love*:
"Warsaw Pact Military Binoculars
used by East German border guards
along the Berlin Wall – $499 –
sorry – limit 2 per customer".
Bummer – which to choose?
He might go ape for a subscription
to *The Potato of the Month Club* . . .
This is getting totally heavy.
"Cashmere watchcap – built a beefy
two layers thick. Never debilitating.
Lets your head breathe, $105".
Ouch. Tempting, you'll admit.
What about, "Obsessively hand-crafted sinks,
employed here as waterfalls, with real water
gushing through them . . . a kind of existential
theatre . . . The kicker is that this paradise
is also a kind of prison". Really.
My dude *has* to have stuff from
Some Like It Hot: Salsa from Hell
or the 12 oz. Ass Kickin' Peanuts.
Capitalism. It blows my mind.
I've mailed my order
for a talisman with his name
in ancient Egyptian hieroglyphics
as a jumping off point.

GERALD STERN
LILACS FOR GINSBERG

I was most interested in what they looked like dead
and I could learn to love them so I waited
for three or four days until the brown set in
and there was a certain reverse curl to the leaf by
which in putting my finger on the main artery
beside the throat I knew the blood had passed on
to someplace else and he was talking to two
demons from the afterlife although it was
just like the mountains in New York state since there was
smoke in the sky and they were yelping and he was
speaking in his telltale New Jersey English
and saying the same thing over and over the way he
did when he was on stage and his white shirt was
perfect and the lack of air and of light
aged the lilacs but he was sitting on a lily
in one or two seconds and he forgot about Eighth Street
and fame and cancer and bent down to pick a loose
diamond but more important than that he talked
to the demons in French and sang with his tinny voice
nor did he go on about his yellowing sickness
but counted the clusters and said they were only stars
and there were two universes intertwined, the
white and the purple, or they were just crumbs or specks
that he could sprinkle on his pie nor could he
exactly remember his sorrow except when he pressed
the lilacs to his face or when he stooped
to bury himself in the bush, then for a moment
he almost did, for lilacs clear the mind
and all the elaborations are possible in their
dear smell and even his death which was so
good and thoughtful became, for a moment, sorrowful.

KAREN VOLKMAN
WELL, YOU NEEDN'T

In discord this incipience, disregard.
You are unhappy with the slant of the windows.
You eat an egg for breakfast, and are ungrateful.
Your hair is a black and gray wing that could be clipped.

I'm not the necessary angel.
My coffee is hot and bitter and so I like it.
Hunter-red your jacket, visible rube.
You know one, two, three, five things and like to sing them.

A mattress on the floor, a cork beneath the chair.
What do you know about comings and goings?
Speak to me sweetly of the smoothness of skins.
No light, no moon, no morning asks our opinion.

Spruce tree, white pine, where do you list?
What am I doing and whom do I move?
One, two, three blue blankets warm my darling.
Ten, twenty, thirty red kisses send him home.

I'm beginning to wonder if love's just a blunder.
Split moon, preacher, of an evening, in a mist.
My coat, bruise-purple, is a visible ruse.
Spruce tree, vagrant, where do you list?

EMILY GROSHOLZ
WHAT REMBRANDT SAW
Portrait of Hendrickje Stoffels, National Gallery, London

The light tug of a pearl drop on her earlobe,
tick of its pendulum against her throat
measuring time's passage, or its sheer
arrest. Here. Again, here.

The weight of two gold necklaces her breast
warms slightly, drape incurved along a swell,
a lapse, a swell. So might he ride,
sails furled, one summer evening on the river.

How fur on flesh is smooth and irritant.
How folds conceal by ivory *impasto*,
display by contour's tributary shadow,
rill of the dark surround.

One hand expressive, one hand self-enclosed.
Lips I have never kissed.
And that inquiring gaze: unasked, unanswered
questions so apparent in the eye.

So shadowy. A pearl
hangs spinning in the balance, like a world.

A. R. AMMONS
DIFFIDENT DANDY

I can't have what I want and wouldn't
want it if I had it:
            this condition
makes flotation widespread: stumps
rise out of their roofs and stones
        amble hills:

maybe I really *don't* want
what I want
        or my deep friendlies would
make me get it:

anyhow, some of the sizable slope stones,
even boulders, have been penned in

by rim-staking saplings come up
                so
no big loosening can slurp downhill:
(a great one could
        lay down a sweep,

oak and hickory flipped flat
like weeds)

I want to see water trickling over
dense grain,
soaked moss letting go discrete drops

I want that – that must be what I want –
while my wants cringe deeper out of sight.

One Hundred Per Cent Ironic

by Ian Gregson

KENNETH KOCH

One Train

Carcanet, £7.95
ISBN 1 85754 269 X

TO READ KENNETH Koch's 'A Time Zone' is to be reminded of what it was like, twenty years ago and more, to be excited by the poets of the New York school. Enjoying them probably also meant you disliked early Heaney, his rural settings and "organic" ideology. You might grudgingly respect Larkin but you'd dislike the way his poems mostly went through the same pattern of development, beginning with a realist notating of an English regional setting, evoking some (usually defeated) characters, making some (usually glum) generalisations about Life, and then opening out into a metaphoric climax involving imagery of larger spaces. By contrast Frank O'Hara, John Ashbery, James Schuyler and Kenneth Koch had been writing – even as early as the 50s – with an ironic verve that constantly questioned and subverted what poetry was supposed to do.

'Time Zone' ends with a memory of Koch writing a poem which "doesn't make too much sense", but the apparent ruefulness of that is undercut because it refers to the whole New York program of asking how much sense you're making as you're trying to make it. Koch is mocking the avant-garde earnestness that lay behind his earlier self's eschewal of poems that made more obvious sense than he thought they should, of an establishment poetic that wanted to monopolise what kind of sense poems should make. But the poem is so attractive because it reinvents O'Hara's "Personism" in order to recreate what it was like to be around the O'Hara

circle in the 50's. "Personism" was a joke manifesto O'Hara wrote one day when he wanted to write a poem to a friend but decided he could just phone him up instead: the poetic associated with it is appropriate for 'Time Zone' because it emphasises inter-relationships and evokes friendships that begin and are sustained by talking and having fun in a metropolitan environment. So Koch describes the meeting of John Ashbery and the artist Jane Freilicher – it's as if "they'd both been thrown into a swimming pool"

> Afloat with ironies jokes sensitivities perceptions and
> sweet swift sophistications
> Like the orchids of Xochimilco a tourist attraction
> for the nations
> Jane is filled with excitement and
> one hundred per cent ironic
> This conversation is joy is speed is
> infinite gin and tonic

This combines the interest of literary biography – it's interesting to hear that the young John Ashbery was "shy and skinny" – with that of poetic parody that rethinks what Personism achieved.

This hints at Koch's particular strength. Clearly the New York poetic was about sophisticated scepticism, about standing to one side of conventional assumptions and being ironic about them. Koch does this, but he also stands to one side of this stance, and is ironic about irony – as that remark about his poem not making "too much sense" shows. This means that he's kept a much more open mind than Ashbery. So he's still writing poems that are, in the New York vein, self-reflexive parodies, for example, of guide books or art criticism. These now seem a dead end, even if they have their worthwhile moments of humour, as in 'Aesthetics of Being in Haiti':

> Don't take off
> With a Zombie
> On a barge
> In the heavy rain.

Koch was always the funniest of the New York poets. Most crucially, though, he's not been content with humour and irony and this has meant he has not got stuck in self-reflexiveness. His retention of an open mind has meant that he has continued to experiment and this has involved finding different ways of making sense – rather than, like Ashbery, endlessly pointing out that the whole notion of "sense" has always to be questioned.

This means that he can explore, in the title poem, the ideas of hidden meanings and of latent potential and suggest, through a series of defamiliarising strategies and images, that there are hidden riches, and more kinds of sense in our experience than we routinely realise. It means that he can retell the classical myth of Io, in a parody of poetic translation, and so invent a kind of postmodernist light verse ("The King of Gods espying her, in her bodacious tresses, / Desired for to fuck with her beside

the watercresses"). Most surprising of all it means that he can occasionally write with a deliberate simplicity and directness, as in "Talking to Patrizia" where he reports a conversation about love between himself and a youngish lesbian. Lines of dialogue are made to straddle the short lines and six-line stanzas, so that the clichés of this kind of dialogue are refreshed, and the baffled earnestness that lies behind their attempt to understand love is revealed:

> I'm sorry I said Patrizia to be so
> Boring I can't stop talking Forgive
> Me. It doesn't bore me at all
> Patrizia says It's my favourite subject
> It isn't every day one sees somebody
> In such a state you can help him by talking to stay
> > alive

Macho Mawkishness

by James Keery

C. K. WILLIAMS
The Vigil

Bloodaxe, £7.95
ISBN 0 85646 269 1

BORN IN NEWARK, New Jersey in 1936, C[harles] K[enneth] Williams graduated from the University of Pennsylvania in 1959 as a beatnik protest poet in the making, and his work of the sixties and seventies goes for the throat. In "an age / of such bestial death", the poet begs forgiveness for "days wasted in no pain" and helps himself without a qualm to that of "lists of victims". Should I ever edit *The Penguin Book of Ignominious Verse*, 'The Beginning of April' will take pride of place:

> I feel terribly strong today...
> I could smash bricks with my bare hands
> or screw
> until I was half out of my mind
>
> the only trouble
> jesus the only trouble
> is I keep thinking about a kid I saw starving on
> > television
> last night from Biafra...

Such an amalgam of appropriated suffering and grotesque sexuality is typical of the "bad shit" in Williams's first two collections, *Lies* (1969) and *I Am the Bitter Name* (1973): "men / who ooze their penises out like snail / feet whose testicles clang in their scrotums women / are like anvils to them"; "the cunts of the mothers the cunts / of the bad daughters stinking / of police stations ... I'm bleeding saying cunt cunt / where is forgiveness?" 'A Day for Anne Frank' imagines "the little gestapo children ... coming home so filthy stinking // of jew's hair"; and finds this to say to the murdered child: "Little Sister, / you are a clot / in the snow, / blackened, / a chunk of phlegm / or puke .. ." It makes you wonder what the poet could have thought he was doing. A poem such as this adds insult to atrocity.

Discernible, just, through the foul-mouthed blatancy is the influence of Robert Bly, before his talent ran to seed an admirable poet. Despite its share of self-righteous pronouncements – "No-one in business can be a Christian" – *The Light Around the Body* (1967) remains a powerful and coherent book. After all, it ought to be possible to be angry in poetry about political injustice, as Bly is, in 'Driving through Minnesota during the Hanoi Bombings' and, with eloquent bewilderment, in 'Sleet Storm on the Merritt Parkway'. His fusion of indignation with surreal irony results in the strangest and profoundest political writing of the age:

> The State Department floats in the heavy jellies near
> > the bottom
> Like exhausted crustaceans, like squids who are

confused,
Sending out beams of black light to the open sea ...

Williams can't match that, admittedly, but in such longer-lined poems as 'In There', 'Dimensions', 'Of What is Past' and 'Patience Is When You Stop Waiting' he adopts Bly's grave oracular rhythms to memorable effect:

Tell me again about silence ... The night is dying.
Wisely it thinks of death as a thing born of desire.

In his third collection, *With Ignorance*, Williams begins to deploy "the line of roughly ten metrical feet which makes his current work immediately recognizable on the page". Michael Donaghy's description is not strictly accurate, for what makes a page of Williams immediately recognizable is the way each line is broken in two at a justified right hand margin. The inference that this is a deliberate policy finds confirmation in the layout of 'Tasks' as printed in *Poetry Review* Vol 81 No 1, where several lines that could comfortably have been accommodated without a break are printed so as to conform to the pattern. Williams has chosen to avoid either the unevenness of occasional unbroken lines or, given a wide-enough page, unbroken blocks of text (contrast *The Butchers of Hull* by Peter Didsbury, another non-standard-width production in which some extremely long lines are, without exception, printed unbroken). Metrical feet have nothing to do with it, least of all the iambics in which Donaghy appears to be reckoning, despite his reference to "amplified free verse"; there are, inevitably, pentameters within the twenty-odd syllable lines, but the characteristic feel, especially in *A Vigil*, is of sprung hexameters, with their combinations of dactyls, anapaests and spondees:

Back bent, knees shattered, teeth rotting; fever and
lesion, the physical
knowledge of evil;
illiterate, numb, insensible, superstitious, lurching
from lust to hunger
to unnameable dread;
the true history I inhabit, its sea of suffering, its wave
to which I am
froth, scum.

Donaghy finds in Williams "a more complex sensibility" than that of Whitman, but for all his psychological knowingness, his insights tend to take the suspect form of binary oppositions ("though he claims he hates her still, I can tell he really loves her and is obsessed by her"). The simple dialectic of epiphanic afflatus ("the scent of roses ... numinous, limpid, abundant, / whose serenity lifts and enfolds me") and ebb-tide abjection ("I am ... scum") is characteristic of both poets:

As I ebb'd with the ocean of life ...
Fascinated, my eyes reverting from the south, dropt,
to follow those slender windrows,
Chaff, straw, splinters of wood, weeds, and the sea-
gluten,
Scum, scales from shining rocks, leaves of salt-
lettuce, left by the tide ...
I too signify at the utmost a little wash'd-up drift ...

Metrically, Whitman's verse is much less hexamet-ric, and there is a greater variety of line-length; one of its formal glories (emulated by Ginsberg) is the occasional line that needs to be broken no less than *four* times to fit the standard Everyman edition. Yet many of Williams's lines might have been plucked from *Leaves of Grass*:

My face beneath your face, face of grief, countenance
of loss, of fear, of irrevocable extinction;
matrix laid upon matrix, mystery on mystery, guise
upon guise, semblance, effigy, likeness.

Like Whitman, Williams frequently crosses the line between psalmodic repetition, a mode in which whole poems are constructed, and mere tautology ("a breeze of benevolent clemency") or versified Roget: "Ineffable, vague, elusive, uncertain, distracted: shouldn't grief have a / form of its own ...?" The immediate reference of the title is to a down-and-out ("Her vigil, somewhere, I know, continues"), but it also invokes both the dithyram-bic ostentation of *A Dream of Mind* ("My vigilance never flags .. . I behold the infernal beholder, I behold/ the uncanny beheld") and 'Vigil Strange', in which Whitman passes "immortal and mystic hours" in a "vigil of night and battlefield dim ..."

There is, however, another source of some of the long, clause-ridden, self-qualifying lines, namely the prose of Henry James, in whose accents the poet contemplates his son's sneakers, "tipped on their sides, still tied, the soles barely scuffed since we just / bought them today, / or rather submitted to Jed's picking them out, to his absolutely having to have them..." In this vein, though in his own accent,

Williams writes his most successful poems, such as 'The Lover', in which the poet's wife is unable to forgive the "abrasive" lover of a dinner-guest and long-standing friend, "not for having caused the husband to switch gender prefer / -ence, but for being, / she must have said, or sighed, a thousand times, so difficult to be with, / so crude, so *tiresome*". The intriguing *donnée* raises the poem above the level of garrulous anecdote on which the poet tends to operate, but it is even more exceptional in not being pressed beyond its narrative and social "intricacies" into the realms of the circumambient gas.

Williams's last lines are much given to *symboliste* and transcendental tropes such as "the perfume of our consternation", "cycles of transfiguration and soaring", "still oak, though, still rose, still world"; and obsessively inclusive gestures, working the word "all" ("like earth, fire, air, from which all beauty must be evolved"; "obliterate all, all madness, all mourning"; "its partial beauties, its imperfect affections, all severed, all torn") to its last gasp. In this context, the last line of 'The Lover' is outstanding in its weight and wit, its affectionate exasperation with a real person:

What after all did she expect of him? Shyness? Diffi-
dence? The diffidence of what? A bride?
In 'Dominion: Depression', in which "hundreds of locusts ... locked in a slow sexual seizure ... seethe

like a single being", the excellent descriptive writing is ruined by the unseemly rush to significance: "so unlike me but like me ... why do they seem such a denial ...?" 'Fragment' moves rather more convincingly from the dying words of a clerk shot in a hold-up to "the irrevocability of death ... a voice that / knew it was dying, / knew it was being – horrible slaughtered, all that it knew and aspired / to instantly voided ..." But the interpolation of "horrible" is part of a systematic forcing of obvious significance (contrast Whitman on a Civil War amputation: "What is removed drips horribly in a pail"; or Larkin on "sure extinction": "the dread / of dying, and being dead, / Flashes afresh to hold and horrify"), in this case with a calculated faux-naivete: "how much I want to ask why I must ... know this, this anguish, this agony ..." Why the puzzlement? The "bitter hug of mortality" (Whitman again) is a perennial theme and fountain of lyrical kitsch: "how brief our mortal moment of time is"; "the ever-ascending downwards of dying"; "the void of unredeemable time"; etc.

Like any poet, Williams ought to be judged on his best poems. 'The Lover' is a fine one; 'The Demagogue', 'Instinct' and 'Time: 1976' are among a handful of others that deserve ungrudging praise. There – that's the best I can do. If truth be told, I find this poet's portentousness and ingratiation repellent. And that awful macho mawkishness is never far away.

Wintry Speech-acts

by Stephen Burt

LOUISE GLÜCK

The First Five Books of Poems

Carcanet, £9.95
ISBN 1 85754 312 2

LOUISE GLÜCK'S 'GRETEL in Darkness' – from *The House on Marshland* (1975) – is one of the few recent poems young American poets can be counted on to know. It begins:

This is the world we wanted.
All who would have seen us dead
are dead. I hear the witch's cry
break in the moonlight through a sheet
of sugar: God rewards.
Her tongue shrivels into gas...

Glück's spare drama and her emotional extremes can strike readers right away: her technique takes longer to notice, and its subtlety may be one reason her third, fourth and fifth books – *Descending Figure* (1980), *The Triumph of Achilles* (1985), and *Ararat* (1990) – have not, despite their renown in America, been published in Britain before. The power other poets seek through weird words, or through metaphor, Glück acquires through tone, enjambments, white space, phrase length, even changes in volume; 'Here Are My Black Clothes' gets its force from its pace, as its concluding sentence speeds up precipitously, then stops short:

> I think now it is better to love no one
> than to love you. Here are my black clothes,
> the tired nightgowns and robes fraying
> in many places. Why should they hang useless
> as though I were going naked? You liked me well
>   enough
> in black: I make you a gift of these objects.
> You will want to touch them with your mouth, run
> your fingers through the thin
> tender underthings and I
> will not need them in my new life.

Such poems are concise *utterances*, attentive not only to speakers but to listeners, and to what kind of speech-act the poem is; even Glück's many myth-poems – on Daphne, Persephone, Gretel, Patroclus, the crucifixion, the Pietá, "Jeanne D'Arc" – crystallize bipolar relations: speaker to hearer, mother to child, lover to lover, child to witch.

Glück admires excision, compression, reserve – she is the Giacometti of contemporary poets: her favorite words are "withdraw", "withhold", her favorite scenes bleak springs, with distant predators and starved, tenacious plants. It is now normal to trace Glück's style (as she does in 'The Deviation') to the anorexia which shadowed her youth: it might be more useful to examine (as she also has) her youthful silence amid a talkative family, or to compare her methods and goals to those of psychotherapy. "I know myself; I've learned to hear like a psychiatrist", she explained in 'The Untrustworthy Speaker': "When I'm quiet, that's when the truth emerges". Her lines sound, always, *considered*, condensed; they are *sentences*, sometimes, in the sense of verdicts, judgements, on their subjects or their listeners, and find flip ways to say terrifying things: "No wonder you are the way you are / afraid of blood, your women / like one brick wall after another".

But to say that Glück abstracts and judges is not to say she cannot describe.

> We sit under the table,
> the adults' hands
> drum on our heads. Outside, the street,
> the contagious vernacular.
>   ('Tango')

Glück will not present an image until she knows why it matters. This is why her scenes so often recall diaries, or else dreams. 'The Beginning' (from the sequence 'Marathon', about a divorce) begins at a dream of an urban market:

> There was only one fruit: blood oranges.
> The markets made displays of them, beautiful
>   displays –
> how else could they compete? And each arrangement
>   had,
> at its center,
> one fruit, cut open.

Later, at a rose-trellis by a suburban boulevard,

> ...what began as love for you
> became a hunger for structure: I could hear
> the woman call to me in common kindness, knowing
> I wouldn't ask for you anymore –
>
> So it was settled: I could have a childhood there.
> Which came to mean being always alone.

Such interpretations are part of Glück's vocation. Her details – whether symbolic in themselves (the vaginal orange) or arbitrary and literal (like names) – are ballast, and tie the poems and their frustrated speakers to this world. This essentially wintry poet writes so many spring poems (as Stevens did) because she is astonished by *other people's* trust in treacherous Nature:

> And by the laundromat
> the Bartletts in their tidy yard –
>
> as though it were not
> wearying, wearying
>
> to hear in the bushes
> the mild harping of the breeze,
> the daffodils flocking and honking –
>   ('For Jane Myers')

Glück could not know so much about embodiment, desire, or physical love if she were not desperately, suspiciously afraid of them: when, two books later, she declares that she "hate[s] sex", we are ready to believe her, and she is ready to explain –

> In my mind tonight
> I hear the question and pursuing answer
> fused in one sound

that mounts and mounts and then
is split into the old selves,
the tired antagonisms. Do you see?
We were made fools of.
And the scent of mock orange
drifts through the window.

How can I rest?
How can I be content
when there is still
that odor in the world?

('Mock Orange')

Anyone who will not hear the music in those lines will not like Glück; anyone who cannot sympathize with them at all has had an enviable sex life, or none.

No one should begin this book at Glück's beginning: *Firstborn* (1968) amounts mostly to a false start, chunky, unidiomatic, and largely in thrall to Robert Lowell – some poems emanate from *Life Studies* ("They're both on Nembutal, / The killer pill"), others are accomplished copies of the early Lowell's apocalyptic-Miltonic demolition-jobs:

The grass below the willow
Of my daughter's wash is curled
With earthworms, and the world
Is measured into row on row
Of unspiced houses, painted to seem real.
The drugged Long Island summer sun drains
Pattern from those empty sleeves, beyond my grand
son
Squealing in his pen. I have survived my life.

Firstborn also hid poems of another kind: short-lined, as if out-of-breath, deliberately fragmentary, with titles like 'Scraps', and 'The Egg', and cold, clipped aphorisms: "Birth, not death, is the hard loss. / I know. I also left a skin there". This chiseling-away, this search for "gists and piths" (Pound) would lead, in *Marshland*, to Glück's real style, as recognizably hers now as in 1975.

The book-length sequence *Ararat* (the most recent work here) is really one drawn-out speech act, Glück's explanation of her family, one incident, character and trauma at a time. Being nearly without figuration, it relies even more than usual

on tone, pace, and psychological acuity. Here is Glück's mother after Glück's father's death:

In her heart, she wants them to go away.
She wants to be back in the cemetery,
back in the sickroom, the hospital. She knows
it isn't possible. But it's her only hope,
the wish to move backward. And just a little,
not so far as the marriage, the first kiss.

('A Fantasy')

The insistent literalism, and the more often end-stopped, longer lines, of *Ararat* can make backyard observations into perfect deployments of portents: "my son's very graceful; he has perfect balance./ He's not competitive, like my sister's daughter", one poem begins. It is an accomplishment to make such sentences *belong* in a poem, however familiar they are in "real life": more than the more recent, more consistent *The Wild Iris* (1993/ U.K. 1996), *Ararat* expands the set of things a modern poem can do.

Glück's limits are easy to state: her insistence that all things be symbols leads her to overuse "the river", "the leaves", "the heart" – her best poems lean on less frequent words. Another danger is melodrama: 'World Breaking Apart' is a fine poem *despite* its daring title. And some of her poems might be just as effective in Finnish or Spanish– they are too entirely speech-*acts*, not enough works of verbal construction. But these are debilities that come with a talent as unfeigning, as strongly linked to feeling and as serious about self-knowledge, as Glück's. Nobody alive has done so much with so little sensory detail, or made so many arresting first lines: "You see, they have no judgement. / So it is natural that they should drown". "I sleep so you will be alive, / it is that simple". Some of her most individual, memorable poems so far are 'Gretel in Darkness', 'For Jane Myers', 'Pomegranate', 'The Drowned Children', 'Portland, 1968', 'Mock Orange', 'The Beginning', 'Horse', 'Elms', 'Adult Grief', 'Widows', and 'Celestial Music'. And even in her lesser work, in all those (only apparently interchangeable) lines and stanzas on seasons, grief, mythic figures and the family romance, there remains much to admire – much discipline, much linguistic intelligence, much power, and considerable wisdom.

> [Her] limits are easy to state... But these are debilities that come with a talent as unfeigning, as strongly linked to feeling and as serious about self-knowledge, as Glück's.

Nun Butt Kicking

By David Wheatley

STEPHEN DOBYNS

Velocities: New & Selected Poems

Bloodaxe, £10.95
ISBN 1 85224 264 7

Common Carnage

Bloodaxe, £8.95
ISBN 1 85224 390 2

NOVELIST AND POET, Stephen Dobyns is a great American yarn spinner, a celebrant of the bawdy and the grotesque, a man who writes about corpses that play clarinets, bowling addicts who molest chickens, and how "it's time to kick a nun in the butt". Given his attachment to storytelling, you might expect Dobyns to resemble poets such as Dana Gioia, Robert McDowell, Mark Jarman and others associated with the New Narrative movement, but as the above examples should make clear, he is a slippier customer than any of these. Dobyns writes freely and frankly about his personal life, but with the same no-nonsense briskness as when he writes in the third person. It's hardly what you'd call confessional writing: as a former journalist, with a nose for a hard story, Dobyns isn't given to striking poses of agonized introspection. How many other poets, even under the cloak of fiction, would react to a drunk's deathwish with the outrageous irony of "Sure, Frenchie, and can you do it / In the next few minutes? Let me help you find a truck, / walk you out to the end of the dock"? Not all that many.

The ability to tell a good story should be the least we expect from our poets, you'd think, but leaving aside *Birthday Letters* when was the last time the narrative alone was enough to hook you on a collection of poems? And for all the talk about New Gen narrative flair, what exactly was the 'Tale of the Mayor's Son', does anyone remember? Memorability, by contrast, has never been a prob-

lem with Dobyns. Who is likely to forget poems as arresting as 'Dead Baby', with its blind man, both hands missing, attempting to pick up a dead baby's corpse, 'Tomatoes', about a woman who dies after plastic surgery and a face-lift, with the result that her son is unable to identify her body, or 'Education', with its tale of sex, deformity, innocence lost and violence – all the vintage Dobyns themes in other words?

To keep things in proportion, it's only fair to point out that many poems in *Velocities* fall well below this standard. At 300 pages for a mere *Selected Poems*, it would be very surprising if they didn't. If the poems I've described make him sound repetitively freakish, he isn't – but it's noticeable that the closer he comes to undisturbed normality, the more often he falters. And taken as a whole, the first three volumes – *Concurrent Beasts*, *Griffon* and *Heat Death* – are apprentice work. The poems are often short and fidgety, and lack narrative focus or punch. But then we encounter a piece like 'Greedy Child' from *The Balthus Poems*, and we know that Dobyns has moved up a gear. And with *Cemetery Nights* he gets even better. Consider 'Cemetery Nights II', a tale of the fantastic straight out of *Twin Peaks,* that ends with a bartender wondering "whatever happened to Jenny Whatshername", and remembering how:

> For fifteen cents she let him see her crack.
> So white it looked, the wound that would never heal;
> then how pink when she had delicately
> spread it apart with two fingers. Excitedly,
> he galloped through the woods, waving a stick,
> hitting trees, clumps of earth; seeking marauders,
> Indians, pirates to kill just to protect her.

(Women aren't the only ones on the receiving end of this queasy sexual gothic, by the way: not since Tony Harrison's *Trackers of Oxyrhynchus* have so many exposed dicks been waved around as in Dobyns' recent poems.)

To finish cavilling, I should point out that it isn't just in his early poems, either, that Dobyns can disappoint. Sometimes he will throw away a perfectly good poem with a bellyflop into platitude and preciousness. Thus 'Sometimes It Still Moves' considers a random fragment of life – a laugh heard in a restaurant – before concluding "Somewhere it still moves. / I must believe that. Otherwise, nothing else in the world / is possible". Surely this is taking chaos theory a bit far? By the same token, 'Pastel Dresses' needlessly spells out its unremarkable message: "How can we not love / this world for what it gives us? How / can we not hate it for what it takes away?" But these days slips like this are the exception rather than the rule.

Turning to *Common Carnage*, the first of his books to be published separately by Bloodaxe, one finds a poem titled 'Uninvited' devoted to the comings and goings of "The Rude One". This is an imp who gatecrashes our parties, bringing his own jazz and booze, and generally delights in throwing things into confusion. His role in our lives is not unlike that of Dobyns himself in contemporary American poetry – a lovable troublemaker. It's a pity it took him so long to cross the Atlantic: he's certainly more deserving of inclusion in an anthology like the *Faber Book of American Verse* than two or three of his contemporaries who made it in. British and Irish poets could learn a lot from his mixture of narrative insouciance and technical command. "Poems? / I've just shown you how to write one" Dobyns crows in 'Bravado'. Read him and see for yourself.

Passage from Serbia

by Adam Thorpe

CHARLES SIMIC
Looking for Trouble
Faber £8.99
ISBN 0-571-19233-5

WHERE CHARLES SIMIC was brought up, you don't have to look for trouble: born in the Serbian slab of Yugoslavia in 1938, his formative years were passed under Nazi occupation. He emigrated with his family to America when he was 11, and is now professor of literary theory and creative writing at the University of New Hampshire. This is a generous Selected of this much-acclaimed poet, complementing his recent Faber collection, *Frightening Toys* (1995).

Pace the blurb, the poems gathered here seem curiously unaffected by America. Or rather, they aren't very American in terms of either subject-matter or linguistic texture: reading them in my head, my inner English accent never budged. Their free verse even reads as if it's been translated – not stiltedly, but with that odd purity that translation tends to have, as if the messy, crunchy bits have been washed out in the passage from one language to another. It's emigrant/immigrant poetry, the stuff of exile, not so much hybrid as balanced precariously on the sharp edge between two worlds. Everything, it seems, was already in place by the time the Simics passed Ellis Island.

The core voice is that of a child who's grown up too quickly, seen too many things. It reminds me of Simic's famous compatriot, Vasco Popa, who twists nursery imagery into something violent and sharp. But Simic, while remaining faithful to the Surrealist tradition of modern Slavian poetry, keeps the violence in the wings. One has only that child's impression of distant madmen running the world, of whispers around tables, of unintelligible speeches on the radio, of that despairing desire to be a weed on the roadside or an "unperturbed" stone rather than something so exquisitely sensitive. In a revealing poem on his childhood, 'Prodigy', the narrator (I presume the poet) tells us how he "grew up bent over / a chessboard", and how

> I'm told but do not believe that
> that summer I witnessed
> men hung from telephone poles.
>
> I remember my mother
> blindfolding me a lot.
>
> She had a way of tucking my head
> suddenly under her overcoat.

There are carefully-layered cultural and political references in this poem – to Beckett (blindness and chess), and to the "masters" who plot our destinies. But the real sophistication (Simic teaches literary theory, after all) is in the way the above passage proceeds: we start with what he's told he saw, so that the reader sees it too but abstractedly, as in a grisly black-and-white photo. Then follows that appalling image of a child having to be blindfolded from the world, with the lilt of that tiny qualifier "a lot" containing both the horror and the absurdity of it all. And then the shock of that sudden, protective act: the film's reaction-shot without the corpse. "She had a way..." he notes: a teasing, guileless, knowing choice of phrase, the whole made typically surreal and sinister by the shadow-image, the verbal echo, of someone "tucking" a head under their arm. This is a poet who wrote a dismembering bestiary for his fingers; who imagined a fork as the hellish foot of a bird, gripped in a fist that becomes the bird's head "large, bald, beakless and blind".

In 'Empires', written at the height of the Bosnian massacres, we have another glimpse of the childhood that led to the hearty menace of these poems. The radio is on: a speech, "gun salutes", his grandmother swearing violently at the "monster". Then she warns him not to go "blabbering about this to anyone... / And pulled my ear to make sure I understood". One had (or has) to be blind, deaf and dumb to survive – and something of the humour of the three wise monkeys peppers these poems, thankfully. He is altogether much more genial than Popa.

But the menace remains throughout, even in the poems whose imaginative world is a weird fusion of Beckett with Magritte – or even with an American realist painter like Hopper, at times. In 'Club Midnight', he sees "you" as the sole owner, customer, and waiter of a seedy nightclub, throwing " a white pair of dice, / In the dark, long after the joint closes"; or a limp, lost dog approaching "the grim-looking president / Of the local SPCA" with no hope of redemption; or as nervously standing to the side of a mirror at 4 a.m., while time and eternity "Which, begging your pardon, / Cast no image /... admire themselves...".

Empty, crumbling, half-erased streets (erased by a child's rubber, in one poem), are a frequent set for these lonely dramas. Crows flap morosely in and out; forests begin Arcadian and end as somewhere to be fled from – towards the video store, the ice-cream truck, "the plane's landing lights". Simic animates objects with a child's glee, but (as more of a genuine alien, perhaps) there's far more at stake here than in the English "Martians"; the sequence on brooms is quite extraordinary. He makes of this ancient utility a devastating symbol of complex humanity while conjuring their bristly particulars, hearing them muttering (yes, hilariously right) "Hieronymous Bosch" – Bosch being the ultimate surreal-realist, I suppose.

There are Dalian crutches, gathered crumbs, an obsession with executioners and the waiting trench – but also some cleansed celebrations of happy moments that exist for themselves, making love or cooking or lazing under summer trees "with the leaves hushed / Or rustling, ever so softly, / About something or other on their mind". With a bit of encouragement, these few poems might even begin to sound like late Theodore Roethke, equally attuned to the little boy within.

Perhaps successful surrealist poetry depends on childhood's guilessness, that grace and airy accident of very young children's poetry, before logical connections have channelled their deep trenches: Simic's poems stand up there with the best of any, and manage to be deeply political as well. It might not be too critically impertinent to see their power as the direct result of that smothering, saving, mother-smelling overcoat, after all.

Loco

by Andrew Zawacki

JAMES TATE

Selected Poems

Carcanet, £9.95
ISBN 1 85754 305 X.

FOR SOME OF us, James Tate's *The Lost Pilot* is the standard by which all 25-and-under apprentice collections are judged. In awarding Tate the Yale Younger Poets Prize in 1967, when Tate was only 24, Dudley Fitts noted his "natural grace" and "robust amused declarative style", concluding that, "James Tate sounds to me like no one I have ever read". This ushered in Tate's status as the sexiest of dorky poets, a self-proclaimed "goof-ball" with an uncanny ability to break hearts, console, disarm and disquiet, inspire and undermine pathos, and otherwise exemplify his self-description as "trepid riding / Tate (gone loco in the / cabeza)". Fitts was almost willing to stake the entire collection on 'Coming Down Cleveland Avenue':

You even lay down
your coat, and she, in
turn, puts hers down
for you. And you put your
shirt down, and she her
blouse, and your pants,
and her skirt, shoes —
removes her lavender
underwear and you slip
into her proud, white skin.

That lyrical fumbling in an elevator, his innocent risqué, would become unmistakable. No less recognizable would be Tate's more sombre, disturbing vision, as in 'For Mother on Father's Day' and its chilling close, "I would have / lent you sugar, mother". The collection's *tour de force* is the title poem for his father, who disappeared over Germany five months after Tate was born, in which the speaker imagines trying to "cajole / you to come back for an evening":

However frightening, I would
discover you, and I would not

turn you in; I would not make
you face your wife, or Dallas,
or the co-pilot, Jim. You

could return to your crazy
orbiting, and I would not try
to fully understand what

it means to you.

Tate was delightfully precocious and, apparently *sui generis*, mature and even inevitable.

This British selection, a reprint of the 1991 Pulitzer Prize-winning *Selected Poems*, covers Tate's first nine volumes: their spoofs of John of the Cross and Wordsworth, recipes for sleep and other self-help guides, exploded and imploded clichés, untrustworthy definitions of prose poetry and grace, and left-handed tributes to Roethke, Jeffers, Patrick Henry, Napoleon ("a pinhead at birth"), Lewis and Clark, and a "Goodtime Jesus", who, waking up late, wonders, "how 'bout some coffee? Don't mind if I do. Take a little ride on my donkey, I love that donkey. Hell, I love everybody". A cata-

> [Tate is] the sexiest of dorky poets, a self-proclaimed "goofball" with an uncanny ability to break hearts, console, disarm and disquiet, inspire and undermine pathos..., and otherwise exemplify his self-description as "trepid riding / Tate (gone loco in the / cabeza)".

logue of Tate's titles is an index of the literary and popular, the demotic and off-centre, and his poems expose gaps in the rational world where the fun fits, or where hurt intrudes. A mayor urinates on the wrong side of the street, while "the trees are sprayed / to give the birds / a slight shock / to avoid unwanted attacks / on the President". There are graves fitted with periscopes and women who spend afterhours knocking them off. An orchestra maims a small-town boy and an airline stewardess fornicating at the Philharmonic. God sticks up his middle finger, "betrayals are not counted saturday night", and a clam falls from the stars in a realization of aloneness. Tate's anarchy is less nonsense than sense rescrambled, and he throws himself, as well, into the "tropical madness":

There's a certain point in each
evening when I have to put on some
really soul-shattering rock-and-roll
music and comb my hair into this
special caveman fright-wig. I've done
as much as two or even three dollars
worth of damage to my apartment in
one hour of all-stops-pulled Bacchic,
Dionysian celebration and revolution
of this great dull life....

Love, of course, is right at home in this new world (dis)order, and Tate may be the best kept secret in modern American love poetry. Sometimes it's just sex, as in 'The Distant Orgasm': "Oooooooo! . . .I know it / can happen next door (see *Musée des Beaux Arts*) / while you are reading". Elsewhere it's a plea for help, an infatuation with a deaf girl that leads to a marital breakup, or a pseudo-mystical attraction to the thaumaturge Fuzzy Wuzzy. Love is also serious, and therefore difficult, as when two are "proud / that we have finished with / the pure amateur's / defensive circling", or when the speaker tells another, "I know only that our paths lie together, / and you cannot endure if you remain alone". Perhaps the most poignant pronouncement of love is an understated passage from the 1972 title sequence 'Absences': "the days just come to me. / Why aren't you in my way?"

Occasionally, Tate's relentless humour grates, and he's least compelling when directing his topsy-turvy, manic energy to absurdity for absurdity's sake, sometimes trying to reel the poem back in with a last line that falters. He can also lapse into easy surrealism, as in "Time X", where, "His television has rabies, / the bake-sale is canceled. / No more Rembrandt-phonebill". *Reckoner* (1986), which closes the selection, contains a few poems which sputter out of an inability to resurrect the comic or unrequited within the mundane (see espe-cially 'Neighbors'), lacking Tate's usual linguistic runarounds, his laugh-and-cry ping pong games, the dizzying verges of sentimentality. While it's a shame that Carcanet didn't update this volume by adding poems from Tate's two most recent books, *Selected Poems* is nonetheless necessary reading in contemporary American poetry: Tate is among the finest, the funniest, the funnest.

Radical Simplicity

by Michael Hulse

ELIZABETH SPIRES

Worldling

Norton £7.50
ISBN 0 393 03855 6

ELIZABETH SPIRES IS one of that generation of American poets now in their forties (others I could nominate include, say, Michael Collier, Linda Bierds and Tom Sleigh) who are onto their fourth or fifth collections, command a respectable follow-ing, publish in substantial magazines like *The Kenyon Review*, *The Partisan Review* or *The New Criterion*, and pocket the top prizes (most recently for Spires, a Whiting Award). For Spires, *Worldling* is the fourth book, and her first since the birth of her daughter in 1991.

The first of its two parts is about the chain of procreation, about pregnancy and birth, and about the new contours of family life in the first years of the child's existence. The title poem has a simple grandeur, in a voice that recalls Coventry Patmore rather more than the George Herbert suggested by an epigraph. From its first premiss – "In a world of souls, I set out to find them" – it traces the quest of the soul at conception for its worldly parents. The last six lines exemplify the archaic beauty that Spires can bring off:

> Past memory, I beheld them,
> naked, their bodies without flaw.
> *It is I*, I whispered.

> I, the nameless one.
> And my parents, spent by the dream
> of creation, slept on.

The poems that trace her daughter's arrival in the world are written on the ground of this moment. Months before the birth, Spires establishes:

> I know the time, the place of our meeting.
> It will be January, the coldest night
> of the year. You will be carrying a lantern
> as you enter the world crying [...]

The second part of the collection is a miscellany, but it is given unity by her sensibility: reverent to a fault, delicate, awed (with an occasional drift into the vatic), Spires cherishes life so deeply that the hunger for radical simplicity ('The Rock') competes in her writing with a desire to explore all the cross-grained intricacies of a single instant (as in her medi-tation on a heron, 'Two Watchers'). No poem here is quite such a *tour de force* as 'The Beds' in her last book, *Annonciade*, but her faith, both in her art and in the spirit that moves Creation, are as heartening, even to an atheist, as the same faith in Herbert. At times I wish Spires would say something horrifying, would speak of a knowledge of the dark places. In a poem written after a visit to the Imperial War Museum in London, she does. A meditation on the new millennium, this is the grim obverse of the book's core faith in Creation:

> The timeless machinery of the universe moving in
> perpetuity
> but abandoned by an inventor bored, or angry,
> with his invention, our reason for being here
> collapsing like a star as we find ourselves,
> for the first time, alone with what we are.

Unsummable

by Justin Quinn

EDGAR BOWERS

Collected Poems

Alfred A. Knopf, $25.00
ISBN 0 679 45456 X

DIFFICULT, LUCID, IMPASSIONED, tactful, lapidary, unpredictable: these are some of the words that come to mind when reading through Edgar Bowers's *Collected Poems*. The adjectives don't add up, just as Bowers's career doesn't reflect any of the larger cultural concerns of the US in the last four decades, as does, say, the career of James Merrill, Adrienne Rich, or John Ashbery. He remains multi-faceted, unsummable, truly individual. His *Collected Poems* – spanning his writing life from *The Form of Loss* (1956) to the uncollected pieces presented here for the first time – contains a meagre 168 pages; and this is the crowning perplexity: that there is so little poetry; that it is so substantial.

Some of the new pieces showcase the most engaging features of his work. The group gathered under the title 'Mazes' have titles that would lead you to expect abstract meditations ('Spaces', 'Numbers', 'Alphabets', 'Schools' etc.) and that's what you get; but who could have expected meditations like these that swerve and tack through such varied terrain – autobiography, scientific treatise, anecdote – with such ease and economy? Following the unpredictable trajectory of Bowers's poems is the principle pleasure they afford. He adheres to none of the templates for pacing or concluding a poem, with the result that the reader is carried along, uncertain of where she or he will end up. Above all, these are poems with arguments: they propound, contradict, offer alternatives and examples. 'Schools' is about the names we give emotions. After some remarks on the nomenclatures of mania and depression, Bowers turns to love in conclusion:

So let me, in my turn, be of each school
Advisory to love: the nice, reluctant
Stoic whom his noblesse oblige subdues,
The epicurean, studious under his tree,
His love like logic with him in a shade
Passionate yet impersonal, or one

Companionate with Plato, content to be
In one time and one place with the one he loves,
His happiness his happiness, a grammar
Of new erotic etymologies –
Though, sometimes, my complaint be Hobbesian,
Brutal and brief, sorry with lust and need.

The idea is difficult (the first clause takes studying), but once the premiss is established, his thought starts branching out easily and elegantly through different possibilities. Nothing in the preceding lapidary blank verse prepares us for the last two lines, which maintain the objective tone, but are achingly personal. Up to this point our attention was directed to various *tableaux* and *aperçus* by the speaker in a rather formal fashion, but then protocols are broken, even while their cadences are not, as he tells us something about himself – something embarrassing, animal, beyond the bourne of polite discourse; something that we recognise all too well in ourselves, which has to do with our appetite for formal arrangement and poise that is thwarted by the body with its flash-floods of emotion and desire.

The old charge brought against poetry that employs traditional forms is that it falsifies both the rhythms of language and life. It is true that Bowers's poetry is far from the demotic, just as it is far from platitudinous ideas of life. His is a beautiful and startling artificiality, a falsification completely true to the grain of things. In 'Schools', it is his adherence to the measure that exacts the final painful knowledge. Also, in the many elegies, rhyme and metre prevent him from getting misty-eyed and thus blurring the picture. The courses of the lives are recounted in all their mundanity and bizarreness: never does he subordinate the biographies to some over-arching program. As the poem ends, you realise you have floated clean of ideology, that the person's life was like this. You know you have simply seen somebody perfectly.

There is no development in his career. He emerged, as the jacket note tells us, "almost fully formed as the major poet he continued to be", with Yvor Winters proclaiming that *The Form of Loss* contained some of "the best American poems of this century, and nine or ten of them among the very great poems". Nevertheless, what's to be done with a poet like Bowers who cannot be accommodated to any theory or university course on the development of US poetry, and yet writes lyrics of such tenderness, wit and complexity? Nothing, except read him.

JAMES APPLEWHITE
TIMOTHY McVEIGH AT HEAVEN'S GATE

Celibate as Timothy McVeigh in his cell,
    these celebrities led by Marshall Applewhite
await their spacecraft. The millennium comes,
    Heaven's Gate the Hale-Bopp comet.

Paranoias accelerate. Surreal explosions bring on
    the Big One. The chip's in your buttock, they see
you on space TV, crack-shots tracking your ass. Skin-
    heads zig-zag their *U.S.* in black paint.

The war game boys have tunnelled deep into where
    we think. Who imagined the helicopters black?
Who'll guide the U.N. in? Our strength cometh from
    uranium, from silos under peaks.

Fascist militias march this consciousness where my
    mild, mad namesake dispensed his barbiturate
poetry. Surfeited on PC's, they haloed heads with plastic
    bags, inhaling a cometary coma.

Fertile America teems with bombs, farm
    of arrogant masteries, gargantuan as myth.
Some are willing to lie down and die with us.
    Their faith is guns. Don't laugh

  at the embrace. They got this stuff at the country
    store, all surplus. The pioneers my quiet ones fled
trained to kill at a distance. You don't learn to love
    yourself, looking through a gun sight.

KILLARNEY CLARY

At junctures we renamed the roads for what happened there: Glasses Lost, Insult, Why Are There No Ghosts. We never returned to the places, and though our trackers felt they learned our history, the sequence was senseless. We might have turned any direction, since what drove us was a desire to occur without erasing what we'd made.

We agreed. We were not scared; we wouldn't be caught. No children. We held hands in ceremony but were uneasy with it. We each had our own pack. We didn't even envy birds.

C. D. WRIGHT
ROSESUCKER RETABLO

Though it be the season   of falling men
Presaged by crop circles
And compact moving masses
Long dresses made all the more dolorous by dark umbrellas
From these very fingers emerge   pistols of love
Lilies of forgiveness
And as you enter the eye   in this palm
Chupa Rosa   bind me   to your secrecy
Open your munificent purse   hoard me

This poem first appeared in *Fourteen Hills*,
the San Francisco State University Review

MARY JO BANG
THE HARBOR

Where she finds hot and haze, a thin man crossing a street,
nothing subtle in a young blond woman blowing smoke, her fitted knit
suggesting several possibilities but mostly the mouth

at the nipple. Everything regressive feels right
and who would be against a bridge named *what I need.*
Now the knitted woman is fading

into the vapor fringe where three theorems meet, she's turned
sullen and solemn, faithful only to the state
of epilogue.

On a day like this, it's try not to bend
to the negative – just stay suspended in ether's abiding,
forget that you're willow-wed to a father so fettered

you claim he is foreign. Caught light
and crash of cymbals, rain washing everyone back
the way they came, through a doorway.

The question, a doorway. Yes it is.
And now nice the clean concrete – free of dog paw, dirt.
A tabula rasa, one side saying too much. The other side in silence.

Here and there is where the capacity for good comes in,
smaller than the hand.
Look looking backwards, while the going on is uphill, and frayed.

Sun drips its paint behind the backdrape of sea spray.
Who will catch the windmill's palm frond in a summer storm?
O, the idea of order. It will be seen through.

JOHN HOLLANDER
X'S SYNDROME

Phi Beta Kappa Poem, Yale University, 1996

Quinsy, archaically dogging the throat, the whiffles
(Where did they go?), the glanders poor horses get,
The pip (a disease of chickens), the purely invented
Candlemaker's glottis (by Peter Shaffer
In nineteen fifty-one): these prebiomedical
Names for blights that afflict us afflict us themselves
With a charm and a horror (those unknowns! lying behind
The folksy masks of such names in an aetiological
Void . . .) And even if now, with a greater degree
Of sophistication, still named after a place
The illness appeared to haunt – Tapanuli fever,
The Black Formosa corruption, Madura foot –
And perhaps the citizens of wherever it was
Bleating objections (as if Lyme, say, didn't want
To have its name stigmatized with a spreading disease
That probably anyway came from deer on Naushon).

But nature disposes and medical science proposes
Other arrangements of naming: a disease like a rare
Flower is given a crypto-Linnaean name
By its responsible discoverer, as with
A wild surmise he gazes on the specific
Symptom that might be ascribed to Y's disease
Or W's, but given the facts of the case,
Had to be acknowledged as something new.

And so "X's syndrome" – the name of a manifestation,
A race of observable elements of illness
Running together (as if for their health? as if
For the sport of it?); not to be named for even
Some singular victim of its incursions or torments
But for the physician who first distinguished it.

And who was X after all? what story could truth
Tell us of him as a person? What of his childhood?
What beach did he play upon in summer twilight
As the golden sand reddened, grew cold, and the tide receded
Into the menacing dark? Or what fair field

Empty of folk, far from larger bodies of water
Did he gaze across, under a leaden sky?
X: was it always his name? was it shortened from something
Polysyllabic? And what was the name of the journal
He published his great result in? No matter. I quote from The
Paper that brought an entity into the world
By naming it, having established the right to do so:
The patient first presented with longer and longer
Periods of silence, matching the silent prognosis
He was presented with; on alternate days
The fever peaked at dawn or evening twilight . . .
A cessation of speech? a silencing, (a muteation?
– Ha, ha!) that may abate if death does not,
Come first with that other silence of the grave . . .

X's Syndrome. Not ours. The illness is ours:
The disease with its causes and slowly evolving rituals
Of treatment will always have been Dr. X's construction.

But now that we know what it's called, we should be well
On our way to recovery, coming around again,
From what it is we're said to suffer from.

MARILYN NELSON
DRIFTER

Something says find out
why rain falls, what makes corn proud
and squash so humble, the questions
call like a train whistle so at fourteen,
fifteen, eighteen, nineteen still on half-fare,
over the receding landscapes the perceiving self
stares back from the darkening window.

LAWRENCE FERLINGHETTI
ARE THERE NOT STILL FIREFLIES

Are there not still fireflies

Are there not still four-leaf clovers

Is not our land still beautiful
        our fields not full of armed enemies
           our cities never bombed
                by foreign invaders
          never occupied
            by iron armies
                speaking barbaric tongues

Are not warriors still valiant
              ready to defend us
Are not our senators
           still wearing fine togas
Are we not still
      a great people
          in the greatest county
            in all the world

Is this not still a free country
Are not our fields still ours
        our gardens still full of flowers
           our ships with full cargoes

Why then do some still fear
        our old world is declining
          our architecture declining
           our art declining
             and the barbarians coming coming
              in their huddled masses
          (What is that sound that fills the ear
                drumming drumming?)

Is not Rome still Rome
Is not beauty still beauty
And truth still truth
Are there not still poets
Are there not still lovers

Are there not still mothers
$\qquad\qquad$ sisters and brothers
Is there not still a full moon
$\qquad\qquad\qquad$ once a month

Are there not still fireflies
Are there not still stars at night
Can we not still see them
$\qquad\qquad$ in bowl of night
$\qquad\qquad\qquad$ signalling to us
$\qquad\qquad\qquad\qquad$ our manifest destinies?

STANLEY MOSS
SHOES

Home, I bang the sand out of my shoes.
I haven't the craft to make a goat's-belly bagpipe
Form a shoe or the art to play it,
But I can see my cold wet shoes
As unwept for bodies without a poet.
I speak for the leather ghosts of children.
I hold one up: a newborn infant without breath.
I cannot smack it into life. I face
Mountains of shoes, endless lines of children
Holding their parents' hands. I hold a shoe to my ear
Like a seashell – hear a child's voice: *God is the old woman*
Who lived in a shoe, she had so many children
She didn't know what to do. I hear the cries of cattle
Begging for mercy in the slaughter-houses,
I smell the stink of the tannery.
I am a shoemaker, not a bard.

Explaining America

by Michael Hulse

ROBERT PINSKY

The Figured Wheel:
New and Collected Poems, 1966-1996

Carcanet, £12.95
ISBN 1 85754 298 3

SINCE LAST AUTUMN, Robert Pinsky, now in his mid-fifties, has been America's Poet Laureate (as the poetry consultant to the Library of Congress has been known for some years), and you might be forgiven for thinking that the poet who, in the opening stages of his career, wrote a book-length verse essay titled *An Explanation of America* was predestined for the office. You might also be forgiven for finding that title both dull and forbidding. In fact, the *Explanation* not only remains at the heart of Pinsky's own work, as the Carcanet blurb rightly declares, but has been coming increasingly, the longer we've lived with it, to occupy a central place in American poetry of this last quarter of the century. It is important to be familiar with it.

I remember my first acquaintance with the poem, and indeed with the name of Pinsky, very clearly. In January 1977, *Agenda* ran a U.S. feature that included the first two sections of Part Two of the *Explanation of America*, which is headed 'Its Great Emptiness'. Too attuned at the time to the different imperious musicks of Rilke and of Pound, I found it difficult to respond to Pinsky's understated but majestically-imagined scruple, that monumental yet conversational quietness of tone that is now the very thing that moves me:

Imagine a child from Virginia or New Hampshire
Alone on the prairie eighty years ago
Or more, one afternoon – the shaggy pelt
Of grasses, for the first time in that child's life,
Flowing for miles. Imagine the moving shadow
Of a cloud far off across that shadeless ocean,
The obliterating strangeness like a tide
That pulls or empties the bubble of the child's
Imaginary heart. No hills, no trees.

Pinsky's perception of Americans as "strangers in a place we must imagine" leads in the second section

to a startling compass of address (you try pitching a poem to your fellow English, Scotch, Welsh, Irish or whoever and see how it feels):

Americans, we choose to see ourselves
As here, yet not here yet – as if a Roman
In mid-Rome should inquire the way to Rome.
Like Jews or Indians, roving on the plains
Of places taken from us, or imagined,
We accumulate the customs, music, words
Of different climates, neighbors and oppressors,
Making encampment in the sand or snow.

These lines are characteristic of the *Explanation*, not only in their essayistic tone, the confident appropriation of a first person plural, and the absence of all the quixotic and anti-logical components of the post-modern, but also in the way a moment purely lyrical (that beautiful last line) will suddenly fissure through the discursive texture like a bright rift of gold in a rock.

The centre of Pinsky's *Explanation of America*, as I read it, is still to come, in the next two sections of Part Two. Following a loose translation of Horace's epistle to Quinctius (I, xvi), Pinsky holds up two Roman models of the good life: Horace on his Sabine farm, and Brutus, in the moments before his death, happy in the knowledge of his virtue and his reputation for virtue. To Pinsky, "the cycle of different aspirations" implied in the two models, twining the heroic wish for republican virtue with the personal, quietist wish for a nest in the country, threads through the essential nature of the American experience. Pinsky is not alone in this view of his own country; and, for Europeans, it is extraordinary to observe its seductive appeal for U.S. intellectuals, especially of the patrician class. One thinks of Robert Lowell, say, but also of the Gore Vidal exemplified in the correspondence with Louis Auchincloss published in *The New Yorker* last year, in which the two novelists agreed to equate the election of Kennedy with the transition from the Roman Republic to the Empire. Pinsky's view is at heart Jeffersonian; but history has long since erased the Jeffersonian code and scrawled less salubrious graffiti across the white neoclassical walls, and the Vidal/Auchincloss analysis, though flawed itself by national hubris, is the one that more persuasively describes what we have seen happening in the U.S. from Kennedy through Nixon to Saddam's antagonists, Bush and Clinton. What makes Pinsky's verse essay so poignant in its grandeur, in other words, is that it records an ideal even as the ideal has been definitively lost to Realpolitik. His America is as Platonic as Geoffrey Hill's England (and the analogy implies what is so magisterial and moving in his account).

Of course Robert Pinsky is more than the author of *An Explanation of America*, and the Carcanet volume gathers everything from his first book, *Sadness and Happiness* (1975), to *The Want Bone* (1990) and recent, previously uncollected poems.

If I have emphasized *An Explanation of America*,

it is not through any wish to ignore the vivid strength of 'History of my Heart', say, or the jazzy, reeling syntax of 'Ginza Samba' (which does greater justice to its subject, the saxophone, than Douglas Dunn's 'Address to Adolphe Saxe in Heaven'). Pinsky is versatile and repays complete and repeated reading. In the last year or so, Carcanet have added Strand, Glück, Tate and Graham to Ashbery, Peck et al, making them the indispensable British publishers of American poetry; and this collected Pinsky is a particularly attractive jewel in the crown.

Splendour and Trash

by Karen Volkman

A. R. AMMONS
Glare
W.W. Norton, £18.95
ISBN 0 393 04096 8

Brink Road
Norton, £8.95
ISBN 0 393 31597 5

THE PRODIGIOUS IMAGINATION and productivity of A. R. Ammons take their latest form in two new volumes: *Glare*, an eloquent, attenuated long-poem, and *Brink Road*, a culling of previously uncollected poems written over the last 25 years. Recipient of two National Book Awards, in 1973 for *Collected Poems* and 1993 for *Garbage*, Ammons is a looming but reticent figure in American poetry, writing in the relative exile of Ithaca, New York, where he has taught at Cornell University for many years. That location, with its punishing winter vistas and creviced valley, forms the stark natural backdrop so integral to Ammons' craggy musings.

One of the disarming aspects of his style is a sweet irony that establishes an airy dialectic within a landscape of root, stone, and stern tasking. That tendency is immediately apparent in *Glare*, for which Ammons set himself the dazzlingly perverse challenge of composing his poem, by typewriter, on a long narrow strip of adding machine tape. (Hence the title of the book's first of two sections 'Strip', followed by the shorter 'Scat Scan'.) But this odd prescription for an emaciated epic ultimately points

up the book's obsessions – with limit, impediment, interruption, boundedness, and spiritual and bodily humbling (merged, necessarily, with bravado). "This strip is so narrow: / a rhythm cannot unwind across it: // it cracks my shoulder blades with / pressing confinement", Ammons grouses, but nonethless the poem teeters ever forward on elegant, spindly lines, the skinniness further emphasized by lean couplets stitched into white space.

Gradually the strip itself comes to seem, in its blithely arbitrary restraints and forward scrolling, a silent comment on the sheer complusiveness of continuance and telling; Ammons' concern with "essential motions" finds an ironic embodiment in this scurvy stricture, in which form and composition are irrevocably yoked. Stripping, scatting, and scanning, of course, are all elements of Ammons' method as he plays high statement and abstraction against a wry backwoods idiom that evokes the Southern cracker, the porchfront philosopher, the homespun metaphysician:

> wdn't it be silly to be serious, now:
> I mean the hardheads and the eggheads
>
> are agreed we are an absurd
> irrelevance on this slice of curvature
>
> and that a boulder from the blue
> could confirm it: imagine, mathematics
>
> wiped out by a wandering stone, or
> grecian urns not forever fair when
> the sun expands...

It may take an American ear to catch the Southern drawl here, and all it implies and entitles. Like Frost, Ammons is not above lulling his readers with a hayseed disingenousness against which to heighten his sense of nature's sometimes ghoulish occupations and inhumanly relentless cycle:

I don't

suppose you want to hear anything
more about me today: well, you know

after a hard freeze, say at the end
of November, or very early December,

ephemerae and moths bound and flutter
about on a warmish day like posthumous

trash: what do these things mean,
starting so late as ghosts when the

hard water is dripping from its
prophecy of what's to come . . .

Despite such invocations, *Glare* is hardly a resigned exit into renunciation and reckoning. The title itself is both noun and imperative, state and action. It might be the other, wittier half of the conversation implicit in Dylan Thomas's rather tendentious instructions against the "dying of the light". And while both "dying" and "light" rank high among *Glare*'s preoccupations, the pure sheen of flux and presence impresses itself with ever-greater radiance on its accomplice and assessor, who can only glower (and "blither") with equal intensity in response.

It is hardly surprising, then, that Ammons is cheerfully willing to give the ornery id its rein: in one section a moving meditation segues into a fantasy of mounting a bookstore clerk, while another begins "I don't actually like the smell of pricks". Aspiring to be bawd as well as ruminant, he at times seems unduly pleased with these lewder maunderings: "that is vulgar: that / is so vulgar:

Wallace Stevens wd / never say anything like that", he writes in mock self-rebuke. But one senses the underlying congratulation at his own audacity, and wonders if Mr. Stevens might not have had a point. A more successful plumbing of the low, in this case low culture, finds Ammons puncuating the poem's sections (particularly in 'Scat Scan') with sound bytes from the American pop lexicon, intoning them like the enigmatic revelations of a smartass sibyl: "WAY COOL" and "oh yeah" and "HELL IS ON WHEELS AGAIN".

As much as *Glare* is an integrated, deliberate project, *Brink Road* is a makeshift assemblage of 150 poems previously uncollected from a quarter century of writing. As such, it has something of the heterogenous feel and charm of a collection of out-takes and B-sides from a legendary band. This is well-mapped, at times too-familiar territory, and in his shorter mode Ammons can slip into an excessively didactic stance: "We might, rather than lament nothingness, / make nothing of more things", begins 'Spike-Tooth Harrows'. While avuncular advice on the subject of non-being has its own delight, a number of these lyric castings lack the urgency and self-questioning that make *Glare* transcend its arsenal of characteristic gestures. In structure and pacing, as well, many poems rest too easily in their deft manoeuvres. In this light, *Glare*'s formal self-straitening is more easily fathomed, an act of rupture to divert and dispel a too-glib fluency.

But as with any work by Ammons, *Brink Road* contains much that is crucial and beautiful, "looking in places too drab for pilgrimage / for revelations such / as the sun's surviving the all-day splintering / of running water // the water broken, too". Exhibitionist, singer, and seer, he is one of the genuine crafters of a distinctly American sublime, stripping, scatting, and scanning a flickering transcendence from splendour and trash.

Cosmological Loveknot

by Emily Grosholz

JAMES APPLEWHITE

Daytime and Starlight

Louisiana State University Press, £10.95
ISBN 0 8071 2150 9

THE POEMS IN this moving and beautiful collection may be read one by one. Yet the more the reader enters into the book, the greater than the sum of its parts the whole seems to be, the more insistently the poems correspond to each other across the pages, as the themes of geography, genealogy, and human attachment grow into a kind of cosmological loveknot over the unquiet grave of the past. The book is wholly dialectical, and the dialectic combines things in a twining more orderly than a tangle but more complex than a mere plait. The homely, familial sites of the author's North Carolina alternate with the universal cityscape of Rome; grandfathers, fathers, and sons part company and find each other again, as past resurfaces in the present; mindfulness and embodiment, culture and nature, exhibit over and over their inseparability: "Beyond, in a dense tangle, fetter-bush twines / wax myrtle the way religion grapples with sin". Living is 'A Run with the Double River'.

One way to describe the dialectic in this book is to say that it moves between the claims that the past is lost and that the past is not lost. The opening poem, 'My Grandparents never watched *Star Trek*', announces the thesis gently and with a humour that makes it no less devastating. Not only are the grandparents and the world they inhabited gone, but so is the poet's own self that belonged to that world: "I turn on TV restlessly, as if to see by the glow / that has cut my life in half, that has beamed me up / or down as to a different planet, while the mother ship / bears my first world from this galaxy faster than light". In part, technology is the culprit, in part, the loss of religion may be blamed. And then there is death, who takes those we love no matter how much we love them. "Those kindred faces / blur into soil, thinning with absence".

And yet no matter where the poet turns, he encounters a past that seems never to have disappeared. Searching "this length of river" with his grown-up son, "Canoeing from one bridge to another. / We reenter those days that seemed / limitless", when three generations of his family were still intact. Looking down onto another river, the Tiber, Applewhite reads history off the cityscape before him: the river metaphor offers him the best way to explain what he means, how "A form's inside the flowing, where the past days are".

Another form for the dialectic is a movement between the claims, "All things are material", and "All things are mindful". But these theses always appear together: whenever Applewhite's language becomes especially spiritual, a material emblem to anchor it appears in the next line; and the most down-to-earth imagery is sure to call up the word that stars the book from beginning to end, "conscious". Thus he addresses the Pope: "And you are heir of all this, / Father, this bliss of canvas and fresco – and the judgment of great / Michelangelo on himself and the race – / this flesh that later, lesser men disgraced with funereal diapers". Applewhite never disgraces our world by covering over its secret, potent flesh. A poem about the poet sailing with his son represents the boat not just from afar, but brings the reader down to cold reality: "I fear our returning through the surf, / imagining how swells lift the windward / hull as we shudder and luff / The wind then topples us toward // a wave that wets our sails. Combers / boil over in their burial of white". Military ideals are housed and articulated in his father's gas station after WWII: "Our service-station soldiers knew greasings / and wrenchings, preaching to me, son of the owner, / their ethic of engines: oil changed for piston rings, / fittings, and bearings, like a code of honor".

But as soon as the world seems like nothing but rocks and stars, kudzu and stumps, broken statues and abandoned cars, the poet reminds, exhorts, riddles, comforts us towards the omnipresence of spirit, of thought. Our own awareness would not be as it is unless the world itself were an array of awarenesses and signals. The fleshy geography of his wife's body becomes a coordinate system, a map, a musical score: mathematical form, melody, "a vision becoming language". Crossing a bridge over (of course) a river to "fetch home milk", the poet finds the air full of signals, including his mother's lullaby: "I hear her again by the river / in this radio tuned to an ether / that crackles with static between / stars from the birth of space". And the changes of autumn are themselves communications. Let the poet have the last word:

> ...These signals relate to one another,
> a simultaneous response to progression through the
>   altered rays.
> Likewise my minds shines back a recognition, seeing
>   these
> colored leaves as banners on the billion-masted ship
>   of Earth
> as it sails in its orbit, with the sun in its galaxy,
> with the galaxy receding from others. And this mind
>   grows,
> like the leaves, slightly dizzy, but wakes to a higher
>   intensity,
> that cannot explain such magnificent, pointless
>   purpose, though
> glowing within this medium of fruition and
>   perishing.
> Mind feels itself turn the colors of wonder: scarlet-
>   maroon
> with beholding, yellow with transiency, green in
>   remembrance –
> and looking into changes to come, a bronze of
>   enduring...

Wanderings

by Brian Henry

JORIE GRAHAM

The Errancy

Carcanet, £9.95
ISBN 1 85754 356 4

CHARLES WRIGHT

Black Zodiac

Farrar, Straus & Giroux; $19
ISBN 0 374 11410 2

JAMES TATE

Shroud of the Gnome

The Ecco Press; $23
ISBN 0 880 01561 6

MANY AMERICAN POETS have responded to the increasingly pervasive confessional mode by retreating into a therapeutic huddle and producing homogenous poems of self-indulgence and relentless self-appraisal. Yet a few poets have worked outside of this poetic climate in an effort to revitalize the lyric poem. Jorie Graham, Charles Wright, and James Tate combine intelligence and sophistication of thought and feeling with formal and linguistic innovation. Their distinct and influential styles have made them among the most indispensable American poets writing today.

Jorie Graham

in particular has established a reputation as a stylemaker and -breaker. Her poetry shifts gears so quickly – within books as well as from book to book – that she continually outperforms herself, abandoning the very achievements that have engendered critical accolades in the past. By embracing indeterminacy and by refusing to succumb to prolonged lyricism, Graham's poetry demonstrates her awareness of the problems attendant to closure, eloquence, and narrative. This approach, neither original nor rare, becomes both when established by a poet committed to meaningful arrangements and rearrangements of language, perception, and the inner life. In the thirty-eight poems in her most recent volume, *The Errancy*, Graham continues to pursue important subject matter – namely the interactions among personal and historical forces – while demonstrating intellectual daring, stylistic bravura, and a serious moral vision.

Graham is not an immediately accessible poet, and the poems in *The Errancy* require multiple readings. With its numerous dashes, parentheses, ellipses, and questions, her complex syntax initiates a series of disruptions that actively work against the poet's own eloquence. Although she distrusts loquacity – an idea that figures prominently in 'Against Eloquence', a 45-line poem with thirty-seven dashes and seven questions – she knows that lyric poets, "wanting only that the singing continue, / if only for a small while longer", must sing, no matter how temporary the song. This disjunctive lyricism – a lyricism struggling against itself – creates one of the primary dramas of these poems.

The epigraph to *The Errancy* – "Since in a net I seek to hold the wind" (from a Wyatt sonnet) – declares the ambition of the poems that follow. Graham's notion of errancy is illuminated by an endnote from Linda Gregerson's *The Reformation of the Subject*: "'discourse' derives from *discurrere* ('to run back and forth') as 'error' or errancy derives from *errare* (to wander) – Knightly errancy, then, begins with a gaze –". Many of the poems in *The Errancy* rely on the tactile and the visual, and Graham follows the motions of *discurrere* and *errare*, most notably in 'Thinking', a revision of Stevens's 'Thirteen Ways of Looking at a Blackbird'. Here the blackbird is a crow, repeatedly altered by the poet's gaze:

> A crow clung like a cough to a wire above me. There
> was a chill.
> It was a version of a crow, untitled as such, tightly
> feathered
> in the chafing air. Rain was expected. All round him
> air
> dilated, as if my steady glance on him, cindering at
> the glance-core
> where it held him tightest, swelled and sucked...

In Graham's poems, objects become secondary to her perceptions of them, and the power of the poet becomes a transformative power:

> The monster of the mind moves easily among its
> marls,
> ...moves gently over the playing field,
> dragon of changes and adjustments,

mightiness of redefining and refinement.

('In the Pasture')

Although many of these poems begin by focusing on a quotidian detail or action – watching a crow on a power line, going outside after a storm, walking along a river – their excursions into territories brimming with complexities make Graham's poetry anything but ordinary. Her ability to locate the momentous within the mundane always depends upon how things fare in "the open sea of [her] / watching". Because "The eye only discovers the visible slowly", these poems do not operate wholly in the visible "world of things"; yet they occupy and explore the most familiar and poignant of human territory, that "between the pleats of matter and the pleats of the soul".

Charles Wright

has said in an interview that "there is no great art without great style", and his poetry, like that of his personal masters Dante, Pound, and Montale, evinces extraordinary style and originality. His recent poems employ a long line broken by "low riders", laden with imagery and intense lyricism, and composed in odd syllabics and regular stanzas. The imbricated lyrics in Wright's latest collection, *Black Zodiac*, map the various intersections of life, language, and landscape:

Journal and landscape
– Discredited form, discredited subject matter –
I tried to resuscitate both, breath and blood,

making them whole again

Through language, strict attention –

('Apologia Pro Vita Sua')

In his verse journals (one of his previous books is called *Zone Journals*), Wright manages to be intimate and autobiographical without writing at length about his family and childhood. This modest autobiographical stance serves as the foreground for meditations on landscape and mortality. Wright often joins these two concerns, and his lush renditions of the landscape frequently possess spiritual undertones that prohibit them from becoming

> Tate has been moving toward a lyricism that carries the vestiges of narrative with it, establishing an oddly pitched, singular music – alternately deadpan and dazzling, understated and florid, earnest and cockamamie.

merely descriptive, as in 'Disjecta Membra', which closes *Black Zodiac*:

What nurtures us denatures us and will strip us
                                                        down.
Zen says, stand by the side of your thoughts
As you might stand by the bank of a wide river.
                                        Dew-burdened,
Spider webs spin like little galaxies in the juniper
                                                        bush,
Morning sunlight corpus delicti
                                        sprawled on the damp
                                                        pavement.
Denatures us to a nub.
And sends us twisting out of our
                                        backyards into history...

Throughout *Black Zodiac*, the landscape returns the poet to his past, where the dead – friends, relatives, writers – mingle with the living. With St. Augustine's imperative "Descend, so that you may ascend" in mind, Wright descends into the past to reclaim and redeem it and its voices as well as himself: "What I remember redeems me, strips me and brings me to rest". Although he is often the only person in his poems, Wright invokes many presences – Dante and Yeats, Michelangelo and Cézanne, St. Paul and St. John of the Cross. When these invocations collide with memories of deceased friends, the result is a spectral poetry "all about lonesomeness".

James Tate

Unlike Graham and Wright, whose distinctiveness depends in part upon the appearance of their poems, James Tate writes conventional-looking poems that are thoroughly unconventional. His poetry combines a prose vernacular with traditional poetic devices and a narrative line while demonstrating uncanny verbal resourcefulness. Since *Distance from Loved Ones* (1990), Tate has been moving toward a lyricism that carries the vestiges of narrative with it, establishing an oddly pitched, singular music – alternately deadpan and dazzling, understated and florid, earnest and cockamamie. His style extends to his tone, which can be simultaneously hip and vulnerable (only Tate would respond to the title 'Where Babies Come From' with the first line "Many are from the Maldives" and then proceed to a moving conclusion). Despite the hilarity, his vision is tragicomic at its core. Although wit can serve as defence mechanisms for a poet, Tate allows them to coexist with the disorientation that often characterizes the human condition and its frailties, follies, and foibles.

The poems in Tate's most recent collection, *Shroud of the Gnome*, are among his funniest dramatic monologues. The language of these narrators, whose synapses seem to have been haywired, can experience peculiar slippages and convolutions: "I'll keep a watch out here for the malefactors / all the while ruminating rumbustiously on my new / runic alphabet, mellifluent memorandum whack whack". Throughout the volume, he constructs a variety of off-kilter worlds that operate by their own logic, as in 'My Felisberto', in which the narrator's intricate and super-rational argument is initially obfuscated by its absurdity:

> My felisberto is handsomer than your mergotroid,
> although, admittedly, your mergotroid may be the
> wiser of the two.
> Whereas your mergotroid never winces or quails,
> my felisberto is a titan of inconsistencies.

> For a night of wit and danger and temptation
> my felisberto would be the obvious choice.
> However, at dawn or dusk when serenity is desired
> your mergotroid cannot be ignored.

Many of these narrators are half-insane didacts: they possess some sort of arcane knowledge, often incorrect, that they wish to purvey before their hold on reality slips completely. This skewed didacticism could be pernicious if it were dishonest, but Tate's narrators believe what they say:

> I for one can barely tell where I trail off
> and you begin, since human beings are reported
> to be ninety-eight percent duct tape
> and feathers anyway.

> ('Same As You')

Shroud of the Gnome is replete with such characters – a jalopy-driving boat-misser, "a crack squadron of soldier ants", "a jackal-headed god of the underworld", and "a hungry little Gnostic in need of a sandwich", among many others. If tragicomedy is the bastard offspring of delight and terror, then Tate is a terribly delightful poet.

Stitchwork

by Justin Quinn

ALICE FRIMAN

Inverted Fire

BkMk Press, $11.95
ISBN 1 886157 07 3

LINDA GREGERSON

The Woman Who Died in Her Sleep

Houghton Mifflin, $19.95
ISBN 0 395 82290 4

SANDY SOLOMON

Pears, Lake, Sun

Peterloo Poets, £7.95
ISBN 1 871471 69 9 (paper)

MARTÍN ESPADA

Imagine the Angels of Bread

W. W. Norton, $11
ISBN 0 393 31686 6 (paper)

A CURIOUS FACT about most poetry these days which draws on autobiography for its material and voice is that it tries to be tender. Gone are the raging epigones of Plath, accusing their close relations, the postman and anyone who happened to be passing by of various kinds of fascism and insensitivity. Now these poets want to be poignant, at all moments aware of the suburban micro-histories that the rest of us pass by. For instance, how touching a fly's death is, or how touching it was when we both saw the moon last night, and how it reflects our… etc., etc. This voice is so monotonous in Alice Friman's *Inverted Fire* that half-way through I started to yearn for a little internecine homicide or for some lover to be told to "fuck off" instead of being subjected to yet another insightful analysis of the relationship, like the following:

> You glance at where I point,
> clutching book and papers,
> determined to hold tight the day's intentions.
> I see myself in the shield of your eyes.

The point about the "fuck off" is serious: if autobiographical verse of this kind can't convey the variety of emotions and situations which a human life encompasses, then it's worthless. We all, yes, have wistful moments thinking about lovers or ecology while looking out a window, but we also experience rage, envy, apathy, hatred; violence is in different forms a part of our lives. Granted there are moments when violence is depicted in *Inverted Fire*, but this is done only to emphasise the fragility of our lives. Which makes her even more wistful again. And unfortunately, Friman doesn't even write this wistful poetry well: she has no flair for line, metaphor or general description. None of the poems surprises, just as none of the transitions from poem to poem surprises.

In contrast, Sandy Solomon and Linda Gregerson both use the autobiographical anecdote in engaging ways. Gregerson can at times be slightly modish (for instance, interrupting sentences with section breaks in the manner of Pinsky and Graham, and in general there is a very Graham-ish texture and tack), while Solomon is more straightforward in her accounts of the hurts and joys of life. In different ways, both poets try to face the sicknesses and deaths of loved ones, and occasionally the inimical violent forces of history, as relayed by television and other means. The TV atrocity poem, which has the poet wringing his or her hands before the screen bright with the images of people suffering in faraway places, is now a stalwart of hundreds of poetry collections from Dingle to Detroit. Gregerson doesn't quite escape the stock opposition between cosy suburban living room and distant horrors, but one recognises one's own confusion and guilt even while registering the imaginative failure of the poem. And although Solomon avoids the TV atrocity poem, its economy of safety and joy vs hurt and danger is present in much of her work. Both explore how poetry can be a kind of knitting together of the fibres torn by illness and violence. Gregerson's 'Safe' is addressed to a friend who is stabbed in the head by a burglar and dies. The speaker dreams of rewinding the terrible events:

> The tendons sewn together and the small bones
> healed, that your hand
> might close on a pencil again [...]
> And the nineteen-year-old burglar returned
> to the cradle or
> his mother's arms, he must have been harmless
> once, even he, who is not sorry [...]

This kind of thing could so easily become wistful

and twee, but Gregerson and Solomon, unlike Friman, are aware of the pitfalls. By "rewinding" the murderer's life as well, Gregerson sidesteps some of the usual clichés and lugubriousness of elegy, giving a wider frame of reference for the damage she is preoccupied with. These latter are part of the general processes of ravelling and unravelling of the minds and the bodies of people. Having children, writing poems, standing up for moral values in a society that respects only the dollar – these activities stitch things together, create a needed textile for the human imagination in the modern world. Sickness, death, violent attack, commercial exploitation of what Gregerson (rather donnishly) keeps referring to as "the body" – these are decreations, destructions. There is no attempt to apportion blame; Gregerson is more interested in bringing us closer to an apprehension of these basic processes. This she does with tact and grace. But there is a monotony of technique (see the three-line stanza above, which is the mainstay of the book) and a feeling of "received wisdom" to the configurations of the personal in *The Woman Who Died in Her Sleep*.

Solomon occasionally turns the attention away from autobiography to still life descriptions. The title poem of *Pears, Lake, Sun* is beautifully observed. Grammar is put aside and then gradually returned to in the rapture of observation:

> Pears on a sunlit ledge, flashes of lake,
> how the poised world pressed itself
> through the floating surface of that day,
> how the manifest made its mark.
>
> On the peeling ledge, pears leaned,
> speckled, lopsided, more than yellow-
> yellow squared-before an open window
> through which flared a nosy, fluent breeze.

In the context of an autobiographical collection the temptation is to read such still lifes as allegory. Solomon however is more subtle and asks would this image have stayed if a certain moment of personal happiness had not fixed it in memory. And then turns again:

> The proximate cause is gone. The moment stays
> through the world's facts: pears, lake, sun,
> become now artifacts, seeming finer
> than the passing beauty of the world itself.
>
> Even this noon I hold them up to praise

in the face of such brilliant fluidity
now that the eaves let slip their slick icicles
and snow eases again into the ground.

The objects float free of personal history only to drift back again in the last stanza above; they also move from being "facts" to "artifacts". Some of the most arresting poems juxtapose this kind of observation of objects with larger narratives as for instance, 'Tidal Basin, Washington, D.C.', in which the concluding imperative to "look, look" commands us to examine the political structures of the US in the layout of the eponymous city.

Solomon's poetry is refreshing in its refusal to adhere to the usual templates for autobiographical narrative. My only reservation is that while the collection contains many excellent poems, the attempt to give them thematic unity is not convincing. She ends the book by questioning the idea of "home", but there's no feeling that this draws together the preceding poems. Nevertheless, *Pears, Lake, Sun* affords much pleasure.

Collections like Martín Espada's get published not because they're full of good poetry, and not because they're speaking the needed language of America's Hispanic community, but because they slot so well into the liberal masochism which is politically correct discourse. This stuff comes off conveyor belts in the US, and its typology isn't hard to describe: good guys = oppressed ethnic group (substitute African Americans, Hispanics, etc.); bad guys = authority figures (police, judges, teachers, etc.). Mix with well indignity and Marxism,

remembering all the while that intelligence and imagination will spoil the batter. When half-baked, send to: The Poetry Editor, Whatever Right-on Publishing House. There is one striking poem in *Imagine the Angels of Bread*, as noticeable as the victimised "spic" family in the neighbourhood of white bigots, which Espada writes of in another poem. In its entirety it goes like this:

> At night,
> with my wife
> sitting on the bed,
> I turn from her
> to unbuckle
> my belt
> so she won't see
> her father
> unbuckling
> his belt

The other poems are, without exception, rubbish and their failure is a more accurate testament of racial oppression than all the indignant anecdotes Espada recounts. What I mean is that this poetry has inherited nothing from the best work in the Spanish tradition, is estranged from what is best in the English tradition, and so must resort to aping the free-verse whines so common in the US at the moment; such cultural discontinuity is always an index of barbarism and injustice on a massive scale. It is poetry which Hispanic-American poets of quality will have no difficulty shoving out of the way to make room for real songs of praise and protest.

Faiths and Works

by Marilyn Hacker

MARILYN NELSON

The Fields of Praise
Louisiana State University Press, $16.95
ISBN 0 8071 2175 4

MARILYN NELSON IS one of a generation of African American poets who came of age in the 1960s and early 1970s, upon whom the pressure to write from a communal and specifically virile rage was felt as strongly as the cold draft from the shut doors of

established literary journals. Black community was re-interpreted as black separatism: a poet like Gwendolyn Brooks whose entire *oeuvre* chronicled the life of Chicago's South Side from World War II on, with a particular but in no way exclusive emphasis on portraits of less-than-remarkable women, the elderly, the un-picturesque, felt obliged to publish a kind of auto-critical credo taking herself to task for not having envisioned a specifically black readership for that work. At least temporarily, she abandoned the formal, linguistic and psychological complexity of her work of the '40s, '50s and early '60s for something more accessible and clearly laudatory of revolutionary black youth. This may only have (also temporarily) perplexed the younger black poets (like Marilyn Nelson) for whom the complexity of Brooks' narratives, the richness of her language, illustrated precisely a way African American voices, and their way with words inflected, as black English is, with Elizabethan playfulness and Miltonic measure, entered into the discourse of American verse.

The Fields of Praise is a mid-career selection from four earlier books, combined with new work. Rather than arrange the poems chronologically, Nelson has chosen to order them thematically: roughly, the maternal and paternal principles; a multi-generational African American family history; spiritual parables; meditations on the nature of good and evil. Still, the book traces a thematic and formal development, almost a literal opening-out and opening-through its concerns. The concentration of the first forty pages is on the poet's childhood intermingled with her own first child's infancy, on the quotidian constrictions of a young mother's life, and, framing those, on the configuration of a kind of Magna Mater growing from images of the poet's mother and of the speaker herself to a usually beneficent but potentially destructive locus of creative energy, in ironic contrast with the real young mother's daily rounds.

These poems are largely from the poet's first two collections: in the context of Nelson's later work (and in that of African American poetry of the '70s and early '80s), a reader is surprised by the absence of the "macrohistorical" world's events. But the energy and wit of these poems, even their occasional frank (comic) claustrophobia, has its source in feminist writing of those same decades, often perceived as largely white, but including the earlier work of Audre Lorde, Lucille Clifton and Toi Derricotte, as well as Nelson, for all of whom the perception of childbirth and child-rearing as events with histories, both oppressive and epiphanic was the center of a world-view.

There is a shock of change encountering the "paternal" side of this diptych, which is not only collective rather than individual, but a literal evocation of "sky-fathers" – African American pilots of the all-black 477th Bombardiers and the 332nd Fighter Group: the "Tuskegee Airmen," of whom the poet's father was one. Written later than most of the "motherhood" poems, this sequence plots the intersection of three kinds of history: that of the American Air Force in World War II, that of the African American experience as impacted and changed by military service, and the individual stories of black men who flew in combat. The impact on black men of military service in World War II, the segregation experienced within the armed forces, the tragic irony of racism in the lives of returning servicemen, were central themes in Gwendolyn Brooks' first two books five decades earlier. Nelson's airmen, though, are individuated in a different, more familial way, in narratives and dramatic monologues (wrought from informal interviews) counterpointing the daily routines and losses of men at war with the incontrovertible weight of race in their lives, from the "full-bird colonel" mistaken for a porter to the squadron of black officers imprisoned for refusing to sign an agreement not to enter the officers' club – while German POWs smoked and laughed outdoors.

The Tuskegee Airmen sequence was originally included in *The Homeplace*, Nelson's 1990 collection in which it followed a narrative sequence tracing the poet's maternal line through four generations, beginning with Diverne, a slave great-great grandmother brought from Jamaica (and the white landowner's scion who fathered her son). This juxtaposition, with its complex perspective on African American history, also highlighted the poet's stylistic range, moving from the sonnets and other fixed forms used for the multi-generational narrative to the deceptively limpid short-lined free-verse of the airmen's stories. Not unlike Tony Harrison in his use of Leeds dialect in *The School of Eloquence*, or Derek Walcott choosing a speaker of Caribbean patois to narrate 'The Schooner Flight', Nelson demonstrates how American Black English is served eloquently by the forms:

> *She think she something, stuck-up island bitch.*
> Chopping wood, hanging laundry on the line,
> and tantalizingly within his reach
> she honed his body's yearning to a keen
> sharp point. And on that point she balanced life.
> *That hoe Diverne think she Marse Tyler's wife.*
>
> ('Balance')

An entire section in the new book contains the 'Homeplace' poems, completed by a newer virtuoso crown of sonnets drawn from the history of a Methodist chapel in Kentucky, founded by a former slave, who first tried out his preaching skills while driving mules:

> *Beloved, stop your grumbling. Be the stars*
> *what give a twisted generation light.*
> *That's what the book say. But old Satan roars*
> *louder, sometimes, than Master. He say, Hate*

the whip-hand and the yoke. Why be a fool?
The Lord Hisself were tempted, Brother Mule.

('Thus Far By Faith')

Underlying the personal/political and the historical/narrative, there is, from Nelson's earliest work on, a theme of spiritual quest structuring the poems: a search for the divine in the quotidian balanced by a meditation on the nature of evil in a spectrum going from childish betrayals and individual bad faith to the authorship and agency of the Middle Passage and the Final Solution. Deist or pagan in the book's beginning, merging with the ecstatic and pragmatic Christianity of the freed slaves and their descendants in "The Homeplace," this takes an enigmatic cast in the section entitled "Hermitage." Nelson here frames a series of psalms and lucid parables about a contemporary Desert Father within the story of a woman's rediscovery of a man she'd loved in student days, now become a contemplative priest-hermit. In a canticle of twelve 5-line stanzas, she braids the obligatory metamorphosis of the woman's passion with the monk's yearning toward God in the erotically charged vocabulary of the *Song of Songs*:

How beautiful You are, my Love,
how beautiful You are.

Your changeful eyes,
the humble grace with which you move
your hands, your laughter, your surprise.

Your listening silences. Your God, who dies.

('A Canticle for Abba Jacob')

Nelson has written eloquently (notably in an essay published in the *Gettysburg Review* in 1995) of her own relationship, as an African American poet, with the canonical tradition and with the counter-tradition of the 'sixties' Black Arts movement, which denied the validity of a black radicalism – that of the Harlem Renaissance, of Robert Hayden, James Baldwin and Gwendolyn Brooks – that positioned itself as a necessary *part* and *development* of the canon, contradicting its power to exclude their varied voices. While moved, in both senses, by the impulse which led to the creation of a separatist Black Aesthetic, Nelson asked "How can a poet survive such a radical self-amputation?" Her own choice was the double voice and double vision which establishes a decolonizing dialectic with the canon: a choice also made by poets like Yusef Komunyakaa, Rita Dove, Michael Harper and Thylias Moss. But "double vision" is a strength of Nelson's work in more than an ethnic context: it grounds her understanding of the mutual sources of erotic and spiritual longing, of the ways the universe reveals its workings in quotidian perceptions. It is enacted in her explorations of the parallel possibilities of free and fixed forms, in the way she creates lyric which rises in eloquent cadenza from a narrative, and heightened language which is rooted in demotic speech.

A Pearl of a Book

by Anne Stevenson

The Selected Letters of Marianne Moore

Bonnie Costello, Celeste Goodridge, Christanne Miller, eds.
Faber, £30
ISBN 0 571 19354 4

ON THE FRONT jacket of this rich selection from Marianne Moore's many thousands of letters, Roger Mayne's 1964 photo-portrait of the seventy-seven-year-old poet looks askance under that famous black broad-brimmed hat, with an expression at once inquisitive and doubtful. Here is American poetry's favourite spinster aunt, Elizabeth Bishop's good witch of Brooklyn, the Ford Motor Company's whimsical correspondent, Bryn Mawr's distinguished, elderly, best dressed, most eccentric graduate. Turn this hefty volume over, however, and meet Miss Marianne Moore as she looked in 1924 when at the age of thirty-seven she won the *Dial* Award and was about to become that important little magazines's acting editor. Unfortunately, Sardony's black-and-white photograph cannot do justice to the crown of red-gold hair that, in her youth, constituted Miss Marianne Moore's chief personal glory. It does, however, catch the sharp angularity of the face, the set, determined chin, the full lips forbidding themselves to smile, the ramrod back and straight-looking clear eyes that made Moore so fearsome an opponent to the uninitiated, for all that she was respected or revered by nearly every literary figure on the modernist scene.

This was the woman who, in January 1919, responded to a letter from Pound (he had offered to help her publish), "I like a fight but I admit that I have at times objected to your promptness with the cudgels". As an editor, she wielded, if not the cudgels, certainly the scissors and paste. Receiving poems from Hart Crane, she protested to her boss, Sibley Watson, that Crane was "not well reefed", and published 'Wine Menagerie', suitably corrected, under her own choice of title, 'Again'. Most famous of all Moore's strenuous revisions is the expurgated version of 'Roosters' she and her mother sent to Elizabeth Bishop in October 1940: "I think it is to your credit, Elizabeth, that when I say you are not to say 'water-closet' you go on saying it... You saw with what gusto I acclaimed 'the mermaid's pap' in Christopher S[mart], but few of us, it seems to me, are fundamentally rude enough to enrich our work in such ways without loss".

Puritanical, exact, ruthless, charming. In 1922, a note from Moore to Yvor Winters pronounced Eliot's *Waste Land* "macabre" and too "compressed". By 1935 Eliot's acquaintance with suffering was beyond her power to imagine. Thanking the poet for sending her a copy of *Murder in the Cathedral* she was "sorry... that there should be knowledge that would make the writing of some parts of it possible". If only for the letters Marianne Moore wrote to her famous contemporaries, this book is worth buying. Its selection from her correspondence with HD, Bryher and Robert McAlmon show all three in their contemporary colours, throwing light on that most exasperating of Moore's early poems, 'Marriage'. From Moore's lifelong correspondence with William Carlos Williams, E.E. Cummings, Stevens, Eliot and Pound a profile of modernism emerges, vibrant with what was happening, unpolluted by the multi-layered commentary of succeeding years.

Yet fascinating as all this is, Marianne Moore's most riveting letters, those that display to the full her inexhaustible energies for observation, memory and language, are often long ones written to her elder brother, (John) Warner Moore. Before Marianne was born, her father suffered a nervous breakdown, precipitating the end of his marriage: exit John Milton Moore, never to be heard of again. Mrs. Moore retreated to the Missouri home of her maternal grandfather, gave birth to her daughter

and later moved with both children, to Carlisle, Pennsylvania, where she taught at the girls' school Marianne attended in her teens. Marianne's early correspondence gives evidence of extraordinary close family ties. Once Warner had left home for Yale and Marianne was at Bryn Mawr, the family sent letters round robin, delighting in a private brand of language. Marianne and her Bryn Mawr classmates were "gators"; Yale was "Turtletown". Marianne signed herself Fangs, varied sometimes to Barca, Uncle or Brother – always a masculine persona. The mother was Mouse or Bunny; Warner was Biter, Fish, or like Marianne herself, Weaz. Inventive playfulness is evident from the very first: "Dear Biter, I recall distinctly how, eighteen gator months ago on the eighteenth of this month you were feebly but persistently trying to emerge from the fragments of a tiny freckled egg the size of a ping-pong ball". After the family read *The Wind in the Willows*, Marianne became Rat, Warner, Badger and their mother Mole. The naming game continued through the years, as comparatively small events gave rise to pages of inspired description. A trip to England and France in 1911 produced "Oxford for fat rich olfactory impressions... It's a Persian garden in terms of modern student life". In Paris, "The Louvre is full of 'rotten Rubens'. I have never seen such atrocities. Mary de Medicis and Henry IVs floating in Elysian 'deshabille' amidst cherubs and fat Homeric porters". Moore's wit and exactitude cry out to be quoted on almost every page.

It may surprise readers that Moore never ever confessed to experiencing sexual passion. Did she suppress her sexuality? Was she a closet lesbian? From the evidence of the letters, no. Her passions were keen but otherwise engaged. Clothes she adored; to sex she was indifferent. Apart from her enduring love for her brother (his wife eventually became jealous) and a few school-girl crushes, she lived contentedly with her similarly sexless (?) mother, reserving her energies for her art. Writing to "Badger" after a shopping trip in September, 1915, Moore remarked "I brought home Hueffer's [Ford Madox Ford's] *Memories and Impressions*, a pearl of a book"... These *Selected Letters* are a pearl of a book. I don't know when a selected correspondence has made me smile so much.

Route 66 Good!

by Ian McMillan

TALVIKKI ANSEL

My Shining Archipelago

Yale, £12.50 hbk
ISBN 0 300 070301 4

KAREN VOLKMAN

Crash's Law

Norton, £7.80
ISBN 0 393 31722 6

YESS! NEW POETS that I've not heard of! New poets springing fully-formed from the page, with smart first collections by respectable publishers! I'm not sure why I love new poets that I know nothing about so much, but I certainly get a thrill of excitement when I've not had to track the poet's progress through *Sol* and *The Rialto* and *Poetry Review* via Basketball Peanut Press. It's the trainspotter in me, I guess, ticking 'em off.

Talvikki Ansel is one of the prestigious Yale Series of Younger Poets: it's a chance for a new writer to shine in a proper collection with an introduction by a respected poet, often (for the last few volumes at least) James Dickey. Ansel has that American knack of making memorable phrases, which is at least part of the poet's job: "Yesterday, all winter, / I had not thought of pears, considered: / pear. The tear-shaped, papery core, / precise seeds". ('Flemish Beauty'). We need more than sharp phrases, though; we need poems, and Ansel does her best to oblige. Her work has a freshness about it that must be more than the surface fizz that comes from looking at American work from an English point of view. A poem like 'Conversations with the Sun Bittern' would stand out on any continent: "I tell it about the drawer with the false bottom in my mother's desk. / I tell it about the letter I haven't finished, to a person who gave me some diamonds. / 'I know all that', it says, and watches a minnow in among the mangrove roots. // 'You know what you must do', it says, 'you must stop...' / 'Breeding miniature horses,' I say. / 'They are useless', it says." The whole poem is bewitchingly seductive, or am I simply being taking in by the foreign accent, the lack of references to Basingstoke or Daddies Sauce ? That's the problem when you read American poets, the same problem you get when you listen to American Music. It's the old Route 66 Good/Route A66 Bad syndrome, as we critics call it. The only minus point is that Ansel likes loose, "freewheeling" sonnet sequences. There are two in the collection: 'Fishing' is a series of postcards from the country and 'Afterwards, Caliban', an incantatory series of Tempest-at-home images in which Caliban is plunged into the middle of Elisabethan London. The sequences just feel too free-wheeling, too lose.

I have to say that, on balance, I prefer Karen Volkman; her work has a natural wildness that Ansel appears to be straining for. The poems remind me a bit of some of the great prose stylists, like John Updike or my own personal demi-god John Cheever. The opening of 'Strictly Political' could almost be the opening of a Cheever morality tale: "Your Trotskyite friend poured his coffee / into the saucer. We and the waitress stared./ Perhaps it was the proper decorum / in Detroit or wherever he was from". She's also a long-line specialist: "That time, you stood on my bed admiring the winter trees. / You said the sky's queer amber was the reflection of fallen snow. / What good is a sky, I might have asked, if it will not give us new blue distance, if it will only throw our loss back at us, shabby lens." Splendid! I love the way that the poems aren't careful; sometimes when I get my eager hands on American magazines I'm a bit disappointed by the workshopped nature of some of the work, the care and attention to form that people on Creative Writing Masters Degrees think is the Golden Key To Poetry.

It's a cliché more worn than your third-best vest that poets make the world seem new and fresh, and Ansel certainly did, and Volkman certainly does: here's her scarecrow: "A man is not a scarecrow, he / breathes and beats at the wind / with a pair of hands. / Throw an apple at him, he takes it, he bites it. / He knows a thing or two // about the country where you live, / country of weather, / country of bitten fruit...".

I've emerged at the other side of these poets excited and energised, and there should be some way of getting poets like this into circulation in this country: maybe in the same way that the PBS has a translation selection, there should be a selection of poets whose first publication was not in Britain, maybe there should be a scheme where we can swap a couple of sexy Bloodaxe Youngbloods for a pair of Sprightly Yales. It should be done! Yesss!

New Lost Land

ANTHONY JULIUS ON TED HUGHES'S RECONCILIATION OF LIFE AND ART

TED HUGHES

Birthday Letters

Faber and Faber, £14.99
ISBN 0 571 19472 9

AND SO... HUGHES meets Plath and they become friends and after a little while together, they decide to book into a hotel and go to bed. The event is commemorated in one of the first poems in this collection, '18 Rugby Street':

> I cannot remember
> How I smuggled myself, wrapped in you,
> Into the hotel. There we were.
> You were slim and lithe and smooth as a fish.
> You were a new world. My new world.
> So this is America, I marvelled.
> Beautiful, beautiful America!

Plath was, of course, American. Hughes has already, in earlier poems, remarked on her "exaggerated American grin" and her "long, perfect, American legs" which "Simply went on up". Later on, Hughes comments of Plath that she "stayed / Alien to me as a window model, / American, airport-hopping superproduct". When she was ill she "cried for America / And its medicine cupboard". Even her Paris "was American".

Americans are glamorous (were particularly so, in those days): more prosperous than us, more powerful, exotic yet also familiar and on our side, ready to be impressed by us, Romans to our Greeks. And American women? All that, and more. More beautiful, better nourished (teeth cared for, legs exercised), more experienced sexually (they move like fish). America figures prominently in the immediate, biographical context of these poems. And while all the poems are personal, '18 Rugby Street' has a tenderness which is exceptional, a lover's memory of his first time with his Beloved.

But of course, he's not just a lover, he's also a poet, and this is love poetry, although of an unusual kind. It therefore has a relation with other love poetry. The poem is an instance of the continuing dialogue within poetry between the poet and his predecessors, the individual talent and tradition.

The reference to America in '18 Rugby Street' therefore has a precise literary resonance:

> Licence my roving hands, and let them go
> Before, behind, between, above, below.
> O my America, my new found land,
> My kingdom.

Thus Donne to his mistress going to bed. Hughes's allusion to the poem is so direct that one reads irony, and searches for the differences between the two experiences. Donne's lover is the more self-consciously masterful. We may speak of an erotics of voyeurism, the lover savouring the moment, reflecting on it while also managing it, in charge of the experience, taking a certain detached pleasure from it. It's not love that is being celebrated here but rather a cooler passion (quite consistent with a momentary surrendering of control), the temporary union of two adults for mutual pleasure.

By contrast, Hughes's lover (we must speak of the lover in the poem and Hughes the poet as the same person, with the one voice) is rapt with the experience of sex. It's the first time, they are together, there's no slow undressing, but instead, a delight in the energy and enthusiasm of his Beloved. It's a wonder – a "marvel" – that's being remembered.

So Hughes is both remembering his lost love and also composing a variant on Donne, thereby staking out a little bit of territory in the discourse of love poetry not yet occupied, just as (a greater, but comparable example) Shakespeare carved out his territory with anti-Petrarchan sonnets that take as their subjects men and not women, or sexually predatory, hot-blooded women, rather than chaste, detached women.

In any event, it is in this double interest in Plath's Americanness that we see Hughes negotiating his double ambition: both to write about Plath *and* to write poetry. Are these negotiations successful? Can the poems be read as anything other than interventions in the contest which is the history of Sylvia Plath?

The book has been marketed as versified autobiography. The "melodramatic publication" and the "great roar and hiss of publicity" that accompanied its appearance was noticed by one reviewer; other reviewers have contributed to just that hiss, as if enlisting in the publisher's sales efforts.

At last, after an extended period of silence, Hughes tells the truth about his relationship with Plath (so it announced). The fact that this truth is conveyed in verse only gives it greater authority. The language is heightened, corresponding to the intensity of the relationship. That it is poetry – Hughes's literary form of choice – gives the story he wants to tell veracity. After all, would Hughes betray his calling by writing poetry that was not true? The absence in *Birthday Letters* of any reflections on the art of poetry – contrast, say, Dante – also encourages the inference that truth telling is Hughes's sole objective. *Birthday Letters* excludes itself from a genre in which *La Vita Nuova* is the exemplar. Sylvia is no Beatrice.

And so one way of reading the poetry is just to place it against earlier accounts of Plath's life. Does he misrepresent his own role? Is this (poetic) special pleading? This is indeed how he has been read, and judged, although he has benefitted from a certain respect and caution in the reviews. No one quite wants to protest either at his interpretation of his wife's life or (more especially) death, although I suspect that this will soon come. Too many people have too great a stake in Plath's life to allow the Hughes version to prevail without challenge, poetry or no poetry.

It is hard to tell how, in the long run, the book will fare against the anti-Hughes versions of the story. (It's my sense of the relative force of the participants in this contest that the hostile versions – whatever their merit – hold sway, but I may be wrong.) It does indeed matter, a great deal, whether *Birthday Letters* does justice to Plath; it may well not do. I am not able to express a view; perhaps no one knows the truth of a marriage other than the parties to it, and perhaps they don't either. And so, if only because of unavoidable scepticism about the possibility of discovering what the relationship between these two poets was really like, one is driven back to the poems as poetry. Which is a good thing too.

And there is some very good poetry indeed in the book. Sometimes it's in individual phrases or lines, and sometimes, after quite a dull passage, a poem will flame alive, as in:

> Falcon Yard:
> Girl-friend like a loaded crossbow. The sound-waves

> Jammed and torn by Joe Lydes Jazz. The hall
> Like the tilting deck of the *Titanic:*
> A silent film, with that blare over it. Suddenly –
> Lucas engineered it – suddenly you.
> First sight. First snapshot isolated
> Unalterable, stilled in the camera's glare.

Once again this marries a sharp, personal memory with a revived poetic convention – here, the lover smitten on first sight of his Beloved, as if shot through the eye.

Love poetry is not like other poetry. It is part of the rhetoric of love poetry that it should be personal and free of rhetoric. Any emphasis on its purely literary properties, any retreat from a purely autobiographical interpretation, is going to provoke readers for whom the personal voice is critical to the pleasure they take in the work. And they're not wrong – or not wrong at least to the extent that a personal, anti-rhetorical voice has to be a defining feature of the poem's rhetoric.

This whole question of how to read love poetry has recently been ventilated in the correspondence pages of the *London Review of Books.* Dipak Nandy writes, demurring from Helen Vendler's reading of Shakespeare's Sonnets (and Tom Paulin's appreciative review of that reading):

> [Vendler's] entire undertaking is based on a single proposition: the rejection of an urgent personal voice which has drawn generations of common readers back to these endlessly readable poems and to the palpable pressure of a voice which is saying something we respond to.

But the point is: one doesn't have to choose between the personal (that is, the autobiographical) voice and that "voice" which manipulates poetic convention to achieve certain literary effects. There is always going to be this tension between the two voices, a tension which poets reconcile in ways that are specific both to the truth of their love affair and to the truth of their art.

Hughes's reconciliation is particularly interesting, and is made possible because his love was herself a very considerable poet. He is thus able to explore his relationship with Plath in terms of his relationship with her poetry, individual talent and tradition here being mapped onto lover and beloved. His poems respond to hers, just as he himself responded to her. Thus (as Ian Sansom points out in his *London Review of Books* review), his poem 'Sam' addresses her poem 'Whiteness I Remember'.

The Plath poem is calm, strong, and ready to make poetry out of the experience it recounts. The horse bolts:

I hung on his neck. Resoluteness
Simplified me: a rider, riding
Hung out over hazard, over hooves
Loud on earth's bedrock. Almost thrown, not
Thrown: fear, wisdom, at one: all colors
Spinning to still in his one whiteness.

This is a poetry of self-possession. Contrast Hughes's poem, which, while keen to demonstrate a certain empathy, also subtly undermines the rider-poet's own presentation of her handling of the incident. This second poem is about panic. Hughes says that he "can live" her "incredulity", her "certainty / That this was it". He "can feel" her "bounced and dangling anguish". She is the victim, unreflective with fear, incapable of any assessment of the true nature of her peril (she's wrong in her certainty).

But then, at the poem's end, Hughes places a four line stanza which has nothing to do with the incident itself but instead jumps forward to her actual death (rather than the one she mistakenly anticipated when on the horse):

when I jumped a fence you strangled me

One giddy moment, then fell off,
Flung yourself off and under my feet to trip me
And tripped me and lay dead. Over in a flash.

Hughes imagines himself to be the horse. Though the hooves kill her, it's her fault, and the horse himself trips. Thus does the poet engage with a predecessor poet and also offer an explanation of his role in her death. It is an extraordinary poem. It claims to know her better than she knows herself, and to call into question any evidence that she (or her allies) might give of the cause of her own death.

Hughes ends his book with 'Red', a poem about Plath's suicide:

When you had your way finally
Our room was red. A judgment chamber.
Shut casket for gems. The carpet of blood
Patterned with darkenings, congealments.

She sacrificed herself — it was her decision, wilful, and without regard to others — in a room that became an "Aztec altar". This is where, one senses, Hughes would have liked the story to end. Seamus Heaney has commented in the *Irish Times* on the "steady wash of gossip, journalism, speculation, investigation and accusation" against Hughes, to which *Birthday Letters* is a response. The book's great merit is that this response is much more than just a defence.

Burst Open Under a Blue-Black Pressure

WILLIAM SCAMMELL ON THE ENDURING LEGACY OF SYLVIA PLATH

IN SYLVIA PLATH'S novel *The Bell Jar* there's a description of Esther/Sylvia on the ski run. "I aimed straight down...the white sun rose no higher... A small, answering point in my own body flew towards it... People and trees receded on either hand like the dark sides of a tunnel as I hurtled on to the still, bright point at the end of it, the pebble at the bottom of the well, the white sweet baby cradled in its mother's belly". This recalls the rush to extinction, and apotheosis, at the end of the poem 'Ariel'. It also recalls, in some of its imagery, the end of the brilliant autobiographical piece 'Ocean 1212W', in which her childhood becomes "a fine white flying myth", sealed off "like a ship in a bottle". In the

blink of an eyelid the poet goes from "stasis" to a hurricane of emotional and physical activity and then back again to stillness. She is both the storm and the ship in its glass container, the helpless child and the vengeful Lady Lazarus, the beebox and the bees within, the "stupid pupil" of the eye and the eyelid that shuts it all out, the mirror and the sheet, oscillating between extreme danger and eternal safety — the womb, the well, the hospital, the bell-jar, the museum, the sack, the bottom of the pool.

What's shocking in Plath's work is not simply the violence and the Nazi imagery but the way in which she re-draws the boundaries between sickness and health, life and death. The ending of

'Ariel', for example, is as triumphantly affirmative as that of Wordsworth's Lucy, "Roll'd round in earth's diurnal course / With rocks and stones and trees". And what it embraces, with calmness and fury, is the fusion of opposites, a species of extinction that is also a starburst of pure being. The psycho-drama is part sexual, part metaphysical. How come that "frost...flower... dew...star" add up to "The dead bell"? Is this pathology or poetry, perversity or a necessary shamanism, danced out beneath the walls of Kennedy's Camelot and Macmillan's old-boy network, both bastions of male solidarity? Is it a reworking of the traditional themes of Coleridge and Yeats, life-in-death and death-in-life, Everywoman's updating of the agonies of the interior life, or a spoilt girl's cry of rage on discovering that the well-stocked mind and eager heart are no prophylactic against disaster? "Bastard / Masturbating a glitter, / He wants to be loved", she says of death. The penetrating contempt applies equally to her own case.

The suicidal impulse, and those extraordinary things Plath does with it in her poems, remains the central puzzle. Anne Stevenson says in her biography that she had a false self, the "bright, optimistic persona" of *Letters Home*, that she had to kill in order to let "her real one...burn free of it". Plath herself was well aware of the different faces people put on, both in literature and in life. (She wrote a college thesis on "doubles" in Dostoyevsky.) In one of her Journal entries she puts it this way: "I have this demon who wants me to run away screaming if I am going to be flawed, fallible. It wants me to think I'm so good I must be perfect. Or nothing... If I get through this year... I'll be able, piece by piece, to face the field of life, instead of running from it the minute it hurts". The odd thing is that this demon of perfectionism applies not to her work but, in a reversal of the writer's usual dilemma, to her life. Piece by piece she has to bring life and work into a satisfactory whole, which means either vanquishing the demon or appeasing it. Hughes's 'The Thought-Fox' ends: "The window is starless still; the clock ticks, / The page is printed". Plath's 'Contusion' replicates these rhythms: "The heart shuts, / The sea slides back, / The mirrors are sheeted". That conscious or unconscious borrowing could be seen as a reproof, or an acknowledgement, or both.

I'm struck by the courage and intelligence she brings to bear on her life, in a poem like 'Tulips', for example:

The tulips are too red in the first place, they hurt me.
Even through the gift paper I could hear them
                                        breathe
Lightly, through their white swaddlings, like an
                                        awful baby.
Their redness talks to my wound, it corresponds . . .
Nobody watched me before, now I am watched.
The tulips turn to me, and the window behind me
Where once a day the light slowly widens and slowly
                                        thins,
And I see myself, flat, ridiculous, a cut-paper shadow
Between the eye of the sun and the eyes of the tulips,
And I have no face, I have wanted to efface myself.
The vivid tulips eat my oxygen.
[...]
The walls, also, seem to be warming themselves.
The tulips should be behind bars like dangerous
                                        animals;
They are opening like the mouth of some great
                                        African cat,
And I am aware of my heart: it opens and closes
Its bowl of red blooms out of sheer love of me.
The water I taste is warm and salt, like the sea,
And comes from a country far away as health.

It has all her characteristic hallmarks: the vivid imagery, which seems to have been her birthright, an effortless skill right from the start; the ability to let her images tell the essential story (though here they are still hung on a conventional narrative thread); the tenacity to stick to her theme; the honesty that walks a fine line between self-pity and self-aggrandizement; the quirky notion that smiles are akin to "hooks", which we find elsewhere in the late poems; the ambivalence towards those we are supposed to love and cling fast to, such as babies, husband and child, nurses, nuns, all those who might help to deal with "wounds", including her own mind and soul; above all that wonderful imaginative leap from the tulip petals to the "bowl of red blooms" of her own heart, whose "sheer love of me" she finds an almost intolerable gift.

"Their redness talks to my wound, it corresponds". Corresponds to what? To her own literal, hospital wound, presumably, and more importantly to the psychic wound urging her to settle for the white wafer of death rather than the "red lead sinkers" of love. Add a hyphen and "corresponds" becomes "co-responds", underlining the divorce that is going on between right reason and wrong reason, and deciding which is which.

Formally, it's still written in the tradition of the

well-made poem, like 'The Moon and the Yew Tree', complete with stanzas and careful line-breaks, though it doesn't use rhyme and its calm prose rhythms throw only an occasional bone to pentameter, saving it up chiefly for the last line. By the time we get to a poem like 'Cut' she has radically changed her style of attack, though not her compelling subject-matter:

What a thrill –
My thumb instead of an onion.
The top quite gone
Except for a sort of hinge

Of skin,
A flap like a hat,
Dead white.
Then that red plush.

Little pilgrim,
The Indian's axed your scalp.
Your turkey wattle
Carpet rolls

Straight from the heart.
I step on it,
clutching my bottle
Of pink fizz.

A celebration, this is.
out of a gap
A million soldiers run,
Redcoats, every one.

Whose side are they on?
O my
Homunculus, I am ill.
I have taken a pill to kill

The thin
Papery feeling.
Saboteur,
Kamikaze man –
The stain on your
Gauze Ku Klux Klan
Babushka
darkens and tarnishes and when

The balled
Pulp of your heart
Confronts its small
Mill of silence

How you jump –
Trepanned veteran,
Dirty girl,
Thumb stump.

This seems to me an extraordinary poem, a miniature epic, better than either 'Daddy' or 'Lady Lazarus', partly because all the rhetoric has been pared away in favour of an awesomely concentrated honesty. The endings of her two most famous, or infamous, poems – "out of the ash / I rise with my red hair / and I eat men like air" and "Daddy, daddy, you bastard, I'm through" – are triumphal, compensatory gestures rather than compelling truths about the condition of her own life; part threat, part taking the will for the deed. 'Cut', on the other hand, is solid muscle, without a superfluous or self-indulgent syllable in sight.

The cut paper of 'Tulips' reappears, so does red life and white death, joined by a "hinge" (literally of skin, metaphorically Sylvia's own will), and that favourite locution "sort of". Sort-of proposes a likeness, or an identity between two items, while allowing for retraction, a sort of get-out clause, depending on whether the self chooses to walk the plank of that invisible hyphen, to climb aboard death-in-life or its sister ship life-in-death. What's sort-of is never quite sorted, and doesn't want to be.

The plot is carried on a series of extraordinary images, balanced on a knife-edge between gruesome farce and desperate tragedy. You could read into it a history of America, if you wanted to, from "little pilgrim" to the veterans of the Second World War and Vietnam. But plainly the thumb is a personification of the self, on its journey from innocence to experience, a Homunculus which has endured as many lonely and perilous adventures as the Ancient Mariner himself. What's so amazing is the dispassionate yet exhilarated tone of voice throughout, oscillating between a grim humour and an honest despair. It climaxes, rhythmically and semantically, in a virtuoso star-burst of opposites and paradoxes, of extreme tenderness and appalled ugly brutality, exemplified by that juxtaposition of the Babushka and the Ku Klux Klan.

"The balled pulp of your heart" is literally the throbbing flesh of the injured thumb, metaphorically the essential self and its deepest beliefs, wondering which way to jump, whether to live or to die. (In American English, "balled" has sexual connotations; in effect the suggestion is "You're fucked", together with the more decorous and

Marvellian one about rolling all our strength and sweetness "up into one Ball".) The "mill of silence" is again literal and figurative, and again a fusion of opposites: the shocked numbness that sets in after pain, and death itself, milling up life by the hour. Or perhaps we should say a sort-of death, a rehearsal. There's no triumphalist get-out here, no sounding brass, just a rueful acknowledgement that the real bastard is not out there but in here. "Dirty girl" – how dare you talk or even think about these things banished from polite society, like incest, or wetting the bed, or self-annihilation. "Thumb stump" – all that's left of the pilgrim who set out hopefully to the new-found land of love and happiness, clear-cut moral judgements of right and wrong. Essentially it's an elegy for the self, as overwhelming in its own pared-down, electric, bewitching style as Milton's 'Lycidas' or Lowell's 'Quaker Graveyard in Nantucket', an oblique Dickinsonian epic to set beside the grandeur of male baroque.

The idea of death, easeful or otherwise, is not exactly a new topic in poetry. What Plath does in the late poems like 'Ariel', 'Sheep in Fog', 'Words', 'Balloons', 'Death & Co', 'By Candlelight', and the bee poems, is to explore her own predicament – which is only a more vivid case of everyone's predicament – with all the brilliant skills which were now at her command. Everything became a subject for poetry, from the look of a candlestick to the "furious Latin" of a mob of bees, from daughterly love-hate to self-hate to the "fixed stars" of her own compulsive patterns of behaviour.

One of her most moving lines, I think, is "The child's cry melts in the wall" in 'Ariel', which alludes partly to the Holocaust, partly to that Dostoyevsky cry about the immemorial suffering of children, partly to her own children and the child in herself. The she-child that is Sylvia melts, the he-child that is father, husband, lover, man-in-black, is "Masturbating a glitter, / He wants to be loved". "Glitter" rhymes, sort of, with stir, flower, star, done for. It's an extraordinary phrase, "Masturbating a glitter", whose referents are as unspoken as the exchanges that go on in the dumb-show of 'Death & Co'. There's the glitter of the unseen knife in 'Cut', the glitter of "Beaten...starry metals" in 'Balloons', the "I" that "foams to wheat, a glitter of seas" in 'Ariel'. The word seems to smell of danger, sexuality, consummation, but one with only the bleakest of outcomes.

And yet we know she could be icily detached about children too, her own and other people's.

Nearly everything in these late poems is both hard-edged and chaotic, monstrously enlarged under the lens of her ego yet fated, faraway, inevitable. How to melt without dissolving altogether into nothingness, how to believe in tenderness while acknowledging the unspeakable facts? One of the reasons why I like 'Tulips' is because it is so human and humane. She can still show compassion towards herself, and so she can in the mortuary humour of 'Cut'.

The bee poems are also alive with doubt and alternatives. I suppose you could say they are Sylvia's equivalent of Blake's tiger and Hughes's pike. She could let them out and stand back, like the mother in 'Morning Song', and turn into a wall or a tree, pretending they're nothing to do with her. Though she asserts "I am in control" in 'Stings', you know that she isn't, and that's why the matter must be investigated. The poem's ending is a re-run of 'Lady Lazarus'. Throughout the sequence she swings between victim and assassin, virgin and queen bee, not-Caesar and God, drudge and no drudge. She has a "self to recover" but can't ever be sure what that self is. Her ambivalence about the bee box – "I have to live with it overnight / And I can't keep away from it" – mirrors the ambivalence in 'Cut'. "Maniacs" by one set of standards, they are also the source of power and of honey. "I ordered this", "I am the owner", "I lay my ear", "I put my eye", "I wonder", "I am", I I I says 'The Arrival of the Bee Box', banging the drum of self-assertion, which is continually undercut by fear. "I can't see what is in there", she complains. What's in there is her. To get to the person, go by way of the bee box, the bell jar, the ship in its bottle, the life at "the bottom of the pool" ('Words').

Plath's poems almost always retain a social, psychological, even domestic dimension, even at their most extreme. Hughes mostly spurns all that, caught up in the vatic marriage of heaven and hell. Path's marriages and relationships, on the other hand, carry with them all the earthly impedimenta of role-playing and social duty. Where does the "I" fit in? What are its duties to society, to the self?

By the time we get to 'Contusion' and 'Edge' even the "troublous/ Wringing of hands" of a poem like 'Child' is behind her, a phrase that is positively warm in comparison with the sheeted mirrors and hooded bone of the end. In lesser hands they could have been just gothic counters, pushed round for effect. Here they affect one as real. Hughes's thistles, you may remember, "burst open under a blue-black pressure", and it's not a bad description of Sylvia's great burst of creativity in her last months. And she was certainly fighting back over the same ground, the "stasis in darkness" of *The Bell Jar*, and 'Daddy', "this dark thing / That sleeps in me", "Looking...for something to love". We can admire the ferocity of her courage even as we mourn its terrible outcome.

There's a sense of awful inevitability about these last poems, as though everything is fated and inexorable. "Fixed stars govern a life", as she says in 'Words'. This recalls some of the things she says about giving birth to her children. "I'm no more your mother / Than the cloud that distils a mirror to reflect its own slow / Effacement at the wind's hand", says 'Morning Song'. When she gives birth to her own death, by committing suicide, there's a similar feeling of detachment, as though it's all out of her hands. At the same time, being a perfectionist and a control freak, we could say that she deliberately writes her own ending, in life as in art. So there's this feeling of helplessness on the one hand and of fulfilment on the other, perfectly summed up in the poem 'Ariel'.

Hughes's animals are either very alive or very dead, and in both cases they instantiate divine law, or white magic. The uneasiness in Plath seems to have more to do with black magic, the life force flipped over on its back, belly up, unable to connect any more, only to lie there in a trance like Buddha or the becalmed Mariner and relapse into nothingness, high up with the clouds or deep down in the sea, in either case bereft of the means to get back in touch with the earth. "The world is blood-hot and personal", says 'Totem', but for her the only colours now are white and black, the only elements rock and water, the only sounds the glassy buzz of insects, the only sights those that take place in a mirror. Meanings are all reduced to one meaning, the ego retreats into the third person of 'Edge', the moon becomes a vulture and "dead" rhymes with "perfected".

*   *   *

Finally I want to touch briefly on the matter of mutual influence between two of the strongest poets of the mid-century. Early on the influence is all one way. Hughes was entering into the first flush of his dynamic, and quickly becoming famous; Plath shared joyfully in his success while still nurturing her own talent, which was encouraged and partly shaped by his powerful imagination. We know that a poem like 'The Moon and the Yew Tree' came out of an exercise set for her by Hughes, though of course what she did with it was very much her own. Earlier on I pointed out how even such a late poem as 'Contusions', when we think of her as speaking wholly in her own voice, closely approximates the rhythms of Hughes's 'The Thought-Fox'. 'Ariel' too, I think, owes something to Hughes's Lawrencian meditation on the feral powers of the mind. Both poems are allegories. Both begin in darkness, and end in consummation. Both surrender themselves to something "coming about its own business", in the one case "God's lioness", in the other the "sudden sharp hot stink of fox". "Something else is alive / Beside the clock's loneliness", says Hughes. "Something else // Hauls me through air", says Plath. Hughes's fox becomes "an eye, / A widening deepening greenness"; Plath's persona becomes a "red // Eye, the cauldron of morning". In both poems a "kill" takes place, an ego is both concentrated and obliterated, and in the act of obliteration "The page is printed", the "arrow" flies to its target.

I don't mean to suggest that 'Ariel' is derivative, or merely imitative, in a limiting sense; simply that Hughes's characteristic rhythms, tropes and symbols had gone deep into her veins, and that his imagination had in some sense empowered her own. The idea of identifying Hughes himself with the first term in "God's lioness", or as Prospero to Sylvia's Ariel, will not go down well with those determined to see him as Plath's evil angel, but it is at least a possibility in this reading of their assault on each other as lovers and poets.

Short lines, obsessive rhyming, the threefold repetition of a word, as in a spell, these are some of the formal characteristics of late Plath, and very much her own. I think Hughes is influenced a little by her voice in *Crow*, and more obviously in the brief lyrics at the end of *Gaudete*, where for the first time he publicly addresses Plath's suicide, though the context is not confessional, and the woman is said in the Prologue to be "a nameless female deity". I'll consider just three of them.

Once I said lightly
Even if the worst happens
We can't fall off the earth.
And again I said
No matter what fire cooks us
We shall be still in the pan together.

And words twice as stupid.
Truly hell heard me.
She fell into the earth
And it was devoured.

*

Waving goodbye, from your banked hospital bed,
Waving, weeping, smiling, flushed
It happened
You knocked the world off, like a flower-vase.

It was the third time. And it smashed.

I turned
I bowed
In the morgue I kissed
Your temple's refrigerated glazed
As rained-on graveyard marble, my
Lips queasy, heart non-existent.

And straightened
Into sun-darkness
Like a pillar over Athens
Defunct
In the glaring metropolis of cameras.

*

I know well
You are not infallible
I know how your huge your unmanageable
Mass of bronze hair shrank to a twist
As thin as a silk scarf, on your skull,
And how your pony's eye darkened larger
holding too lucidly the deep glimpse
After the humane killer

And I had to lift your hand for you

While your chin sank to your chest
With the sheer weariness
Of taking away from everybody
Your envied beauty, your much-desired beauty
Your hardly-used beauty

Of lifting away yourself
From yourself
And weeping with the ache of the effort

This last is a sort of telling Aphrodite where she gets off, a sardonic critique of the deity's all-too-human ego. The middle one is the best, I think, and one of the interesting things about it is the way its stripped-down shape, and vivid imagery, are both reminiscent of Plath. The key elements are the vase, the marble tombstone, the pillar over Athens, and the pun on "temple". The cameras, of course, are not just those of the tourist industry prowling the Acropolis but those wielded ever since the tragedy by scholars, academics, journalists, biographers, critics, all those who have a theory about how and why the vase got smashed in the first place. As a report from the front of a personal tragedy it's dramatic and partially convincing, but the stony imagery and detached tone of voice locks the door on exploration and grief. It answers violence with violence, as it were. It lacks that imaginative openness which is such a joy in 'Pike' and in 'Ariel'.

To summarise, baldly, Hughes is riveting when he tracks down and exhibits the natural world, exulting in its diversity and mastery, less so when he puts on the shaman's motley and proceeds from axioms which have not been inwardly experienced or felt on his own pulses. As Tom Paulin has said, his poetry can be seen as a species of Protestantism in action, conducting first-hand negotiations with God, probing those "laws of creation" in order to extrapolate and dramatise what inferences we might draw from them about reason and rationality. In his own way, he too is scrutinising the boundaries between natural and unnatural.

Plath is riveting when she is down full fathom five in the floodwaters of her own ambiguous feelings, less so when she is merely assertive and revengeful, spraying anger in all directions. Both of them, in their different ways, touch a painful divinity; and without that poetry is a wilderness of syllables and clever remarks. ". . . How but most glad / could be this adam's woman / when all earth his words do summon / leaps to laud such man's blood", says Plath's early 'Ode to Ted', written in 1956. It's an apprentice piece, soaked in Hopkins and Anglo-Saxon alliteration. What's interesting, is the rhyme on "woman" and "summon", and the awful irony of that lauding of "man's blood", which she will later call for in an entirely different way. I think it's next to impossible to quantify what they gave each other in their personal lives. What they gave us we can continue to be grateful for.

From *The Fox Thinks Twice*, a lecture given at the Cheltenham Festival in 1997.

Keeping Hungry

AL ALVAREZ IN CONVERSATION WITH GREGORY LeSTAGE

AL ALVAREZ (B. 1929) has written or edited over twenty books, including poetry, criticism, novels, and non-fiction studies of subjects ranging from suicide, divorce and night to poker, North Sea oil and mountaineering. As the poetry critic for the *Observer* from 1956 to 1966, he introduced to the public British, American, and European poets now recognised as essential in the post-war canon. As editor of *The New Poetry* anthology (1962) and author of its landmark essay, 'Beyond The Gentility Principle', he was central in establishing a new generation of poets and poetry, and, consequently, one of the most influential anthologists of the last forty years. Since the publication of *Autumn to Autumn and Selected Poems 1953-1976* (Macmillan, 1978), he has been publishing poems in magazines and newspapers.

GL: You are both a critic and a poet. Which came first and when?

AA: I guess the poetry came first because I was writing it when I was a teenager at school. However, in the beginning, they were kind of the same thing. I fell in love with John Donne when I was sixteen. I was at a school called Oundle, where I began as a scientist. I realised within minutes that wasn't where my talents lay, but I was stuck with it. Although the school paid very little attention to English Literature, there was a wonderful guy who taught us English. He had studied under I. A. Richards at Cambridge and used Richards' method of practical criticism. That is, looking at poems without revealing or caring who the poets were. One of them was a poem by Donne called 'Witchcraft by a Picture' and it was like *le coup de foudre*. I thought, "Where have you been all my life?". I didn't understand a word of it, but I just felt WHANG – that was it. Epiphany. Since then, of course, I've fallen in love with many different writers, like you do – it's part of the business of learning to be a writer. I loved Housman, Lawrence. But those were just youthful infatuations; meaning, I find it very hard now to be friends. But John Donne I kind of married. It was a real love.

GL: How did you become interested in the scholarly and critical aspects of poetry?

AA: Forty-seven years ago, all that Oxford taught was the "Appreciative School of Criticism". As an undergraduate, I felt that it must be possible to appreciate poetry, but at the same time to write about it analytically – to be able to appreciate it with "intelligence", and not just aesthetic sensibility. I also believed it was very important to respond to the text itself and wanted academic license to do this. At the end of my first year, I expressed my frustration to F.W. Bateson, my left-wing tutor at Corpus, and he told me to spend my summer reading I. A. Richards and William Empson. I did exactly that, reading *Practical Criticism* and *Seven Types of Ambiguity*, and I discovered the New Criticism and wanted to spread the good news. So some like-minded Corpus Christi friends and I wrote a manifesto about how terrible Oxford criticism was. We printed it up as a leaflet, distributed it, and founded something called The Critical Society. We invited Empson to come and talk. We invited Leavis. It was an immensely lively group. Because the Oxford English Faculty taught nothing after 1830, the Society was a movement in itself. I was very much involved in it and loved the controversy. At the same time, I was publishing poetry at Oxford, quite a lot of it, and that's what I always thought of myself as being. As a student, I had a "good nose" for other people's poetry, as well as my own, and I think I always have had.

GL: In the early 1960s, you made a conscious decision to move to the periphery of the academy and then to leave it altogether. You made your critical inroads outside the academy. What is your opinion of academic critics?

AA: My feeling is that the academic world is full of very clever people, but what most of them seem to lack is instinctive taste. It's second-hand taste. If you meet, say, well... let's leave the names out... some clever don at a cocktail party and you say to him, "Shakespeare is the greatest poet in the English language", he will then produce a series of very good articles explaining why Shakespeare is the greatest poet in the English language. So, you run into him six months later and you say, "Actually, I think I got it wrong:

the really great poet is John Gower". And then he will produce another series of equally brilliant articles explaining why Gower is better than Shakespeare. Basically, I think a lot of these guys don't know shit from Shinola. As I said, I think I've got a good ear – maybe because I was brought up in a musical family. That's what criticism is about: you've got to be able to hear it in order to respond to it.

GL: From early on, your critical work has focused on the notion of "tradition". *The Shaping Spirit: Studies in Modern English and American Poets* (1958) concerns itself with the forces at work in the disintegration and formation of poetic traditions, namely Modernism. Your seminal essay, 'Beyond The Gentility Principle', and *The New Poetry* anthology (1962) concern themselves with breaking out of one tradition and forming a new one in English poetry. That is, you set out to be a critical force behind a poetic movement. Did it work, in your opinion?

> My feeling is that the academic world is full of very clever people, but what most of them seem to lack is instinctive taste. It's second-hand taste.

AA: One of the great wonders of my life, in all modesty, is that I genuinely changed the way people read poetry in the 1960s because of *The New Poetry* and because of my regular contributions to the *Observer* as its poetry critic/editor. I think *The New Poetry* was one of the few poetry anthologies that was a best-seller. It – and the second edition – sold a lot of copies and had a very considerable influence, I believe. But the only place where I am truly famous is Las Vegas, Nevada, because of writing that book, *The Biggest Game in Town*. I must be the only genuine, published poet who has ever played in the World Series of Poker.

GL: Of this new tradition you demanded "a new seriousness" and "a willingness to face the full range of experience with full intelligence". In your opinion, Auden, Dylan Thomas, and The Movement had shirked it. Where did you find the seeds of this movement?

AA: By the time I wrote my essay, I think that the Americans were already doing it, much more than the English. A lot of the Americans were wild, crazy people. Although it was all tweed jackets and university jobs, they were alcoholics, etc., etc. There was a great deal of unhappiness and despair from the likes of Delmore Schwartz,

Berryman, Roethke. The degree of booze that went down was very great. When I was a young visiting lecturer at Princeton, between 1953 and 1958, I was kind of adopted by Richard Blackmur, who was also very much involved in all this. I arrived the year after Berryman had been there. I just felt that I responded to what the American poets were trying to do, while, at the same time, felt that the British were very insular.

Afterwards, between 1961 and 1964, I was doing a series for the BBC Third Programme, *Under Pressure*, which later became a book, about contemporary cultural life in Eastern Europe. I went to Poland and I met Zbigniew Herbert and some other poets who expanded my view of what modern poetry should be doing. As a result, I brought to Penguin and to England a number of poets, none of whom had been translated. I got them translated when I was the advisory editor for *The Penguin Modern European Poets* series. They are now standard issue, but, at the time, they were doing something quite different from The Movement, and it seemed to me that what the Americans were doing in a rather unbridled way the Europeans were doing in a very grave, ironic, less excitable way.

GL: Maybe you can clarify something. In 'Beyond the Gentility Principle', you criticised in English poetry the tendency to show "that life is always more or less orderly, people more or less polite, their emotions and habits more or less controllable, that God, in short, is more or less good". But in *The Faber Book of Modern European Poetry* (1992), you state that the best in Europe is "a poetry of private life, good behaviour, and that much abused term 'decency'". Can you explain this?

AA: I think by "decency", I actually mean moral decency. I am a great believer in decency – more and more so as I grow older. Decency is not the same thing as complacency. I think that English gentility, that aspect I was criticizing, was a kind of complacency.

GL: Maybe I am comparing two unlike points. Are you saying that what is trash in one poetics can be treasure in another?

AA: I think that could be true. In totalitarian Eastern Europe, the private life became profoundly important. It was all they had. Public life was all bullshit and propaganda. If you read people like Holub and Kundera, there is an ironic, desparate sanity, as if they were walking the tightrope. Writing about private life and decency was a means of survival for these people. This was not the case for the English poets. That was needless caution.

GL: From the vantage point of 1998, which English poet in the *New Poetry* group best made himself, as you prescribed, "immune" to "gentility", that "disease so often found in English culture"?

AA: In England, the only ones doing it in the early 1960s were Ted Hughes and Thom Gunn.

GL: Whose poetry was particularly symbiotic with your critical message, with your hopes for the direction poetry should take?

AA: Although Sylvia Plath was very disappointed not to be included in the first edition of *The New Poetry*, I believe that what I was saying in 'Beyond the Gentility Principle' was very close to what she thought was necessary. It was putting in critical language something that she felt very strongly about and which she, I'm sure, was discussing with Hughes. I think, in a way, that because there was somebody making a case beforehand for what she was trying to do made it easier for her to do it. She knew that there was an existing sympathetic critical stance. If you are any kind of a writer, you have got to postulate that there is someone out there listening. I don't mean an audience, I just mean someone, an individual whose wavelength is the same as yours.

GL: You were a close friend of Plath. How do you think she's been handled since her death? What would she think of the patron sainthood given her by some circles of feminist literary criticism?

AA: I think that she has been wildly misinterpreted. I always think that there are two Sylvia Plaths. One is the woman who wrote *The Bell Jar* and then had a famous marital break-up. Her married self could be interpreted as one who was badly treated by her husband, but I am quite sure it was a two-way problem. Husbands don't walk out on perfect wives. However, that is the woman who has become the feminist icon. I think that those critics who cast her in this role tend to place *The Bell Jar* at the centre of their arguments, with the poetry incidental. The other Sylvia is the poet who wrote these unbelievably good poems. I really do think she's a genius, immensely original. What you have to under-

stand about her poetry is that the later poems are departures from the earlier poems. I think a lot of the earlier poems are rather boring. The pre-*Ariel* poems, those in *The Colossus*, are not that interesting. But I think that the early poems were necessary because what they represent is a very long, hard apprenticeship in the art of poetry: she just knew what she was doing. She could do anything. If you wanted a sestina, she could do it. Terza rima, a villanelle, anything. She was just technically able and the point about technical ability is that, as I wrote in *The Savage God*, when your demon takes you by the throat and shakes you, you know how to handle it. You've got all the skills necessary. What is marvellous about her, and what is widely missed, is the discipline, not the hurt and the anger and the martyrdom. Another thing: there is a huge amount of anger, but a very small amount of martyrdom, which critics mix up. The rage is so beautifully controlled. Compare her with Anne Sexton, at her average, who has no control at all. If there's no artistic control, then there's no emotional control. I think that really good poets have a more open hotline to their core, to their voice. Hughes, certainly when he was younger and still now, can suddenly get through to his core. I think Sylvia, right at the end, had a permanently open hotline to that living thing. But it wasn't suffering. You see, what pisses me off is that people don't understand that it doesn't matter how gloomily or ungloomily you write – what matters is the pleasure in getting it right. I was at a conference on suicide in New York. There was a panel headed by a hip psychoanalyst and he was discussing Sylvia's late poetry and his interpretation of it as her recognition that she was writing for posterity. I turned to him and said, "Oh, come on! She wasn't writing for posterity. She was just trying to get it right".

GL: So, you were providing the critical language to an early creative stage?

AA: Maybe. Hughes, Sylvia and I were all the same age, within a year or two. There was a lot of dialogue. I think that the real criticism comes out of a community of interest when you find out that you are all trying to do the same thing. I was writing quite a bit of poetry at the time, but I also felt that it was my job to say what we were all about.

GL: Do you think there has been a true movement in English poetry since the early 1960s?

AA: It has always been extremely difficult to distinguish between real movements and fads. A great deal of writing about poetry and what is "happening" is very much like reading the fashion pages in newspapers. In the 1930s, a style column could have said, "Poems will be long this year-and re[a]d". Recently, I think that the Martian period, and like periods, was just a little fashion movement, like wearing nose rings, like punk and green hair and junk clothes. It's ornamentation related to fashion. The way these little movements in poetry over the past twenty-five years have been promoted is very much as if they were fashion phenomena.

GL: So, would you say that in the last twenty-five or so years, fashion and ornament have been the defining characteristics of poetry and that there has not been a movement of substance?

AA: I think that the idea of a movement is more of an academic facility. If you talk about the Georgians or "1930s" poetry, it's just a convenience. In these so-called movements, what you've actually got is very few real poets and a lot of wannabes. And the real poets may or may not influence the wannabes, but it takes time to sift down. Look, for example, at the phenomenon of Edward Thomas, a wonderful poet who was subsumed into the Georgians, although he had nothing much to do with them. Larkin, at his best, is an absolutely wonderful minor poet. But one Larkin doesn't make a movement, as it were. In the academic equation, The Movement was greater than the sum of its parts. Their association with it doesn't mean that Amis, or Davie, or Wain are any good. You can jumble them all together and they are less or equally good; they are often indistinguishable. The idea of writing to a style is really an academic convenience, a way of saying, "We can deal more easily with these poets together".

GL: But certainly groups do form among like-minded poets. Who, then, is best suited to identify them?

AA: Let me answer the question by evading it. I was the poetry critic/editor for the *Observer* from 1956 to 1966. During that time, the voices of the poets whom I really admired – Hughes,

> If Sylvia had died a year before... she would have remained relegated to the schools of Stevens and Roethke. In her last year, all the poems are about rage, despair and abandonment: and she became a great poet.

Sylvia, Berryman, Lowell – were loud and clear to me. After that time, I was no longer able to listen properly. If a package had thumped through my letterbox containing a new Sylvia Plath, I wouldn't have been able to see, hear why it was as good as it was. For the best critics, I think it's a question of being part of it. In the late '50s and early '60s we were all interested in similiar things. I was tuned in, but I was never really been part of the poetry "scene", meaning the group where social, creative, and critical are virtually the same. It's very difficult to write the truth if a guy you spend a lot of time with publishes a shitty book. I'm no longer *au courant* and could not responsibly make a comment on poetry today. However, you occasionally regain your hearing. Very recently, there was a wonderful collection by this woman called Virginia Adair. A number of her poems have appeared in *The New Yorker* over the past year. She's 83 and blind and living in Claremont, California. Her voice I can hear. Her poem 'Devon' is one of the most extraordinary poems I've read in years.

GL: In your essay, 'The Poet in the University' (1955), you criticised academic verse as that which is destined to be "almost never new, almost always fashionable; knowing, polished, learned, measured, but, as often as not, dead". How did you feel about the fact that a number of The Movement poets were university people? Do you feel differently now?

AA: I was never much of a supporter of The Movement as an "idea". It had very little to do with what I was promulgating then because it was contributing to the Gentility Principle. However, I liked the work of some of the individuals who were associated with it, like Larkin and Gunn. At the time of *The New Poetry*, it was not possible to compile an anthology without including the poetry that was currently in the limelight and working very hard to stay there. Therefore, I had to include these academic poets. But I also attached an essay arguing why I didn't like a big chunk of what I included. Of course, I published the new or unsung poets I thought were interesting and were representative of what I hoped poetry would become. Regarding poets in the academy, things have changed a lot since the 1950s. Then it was possible, if you had a degree – there were fewer around at that time – to make a living outside the university. It was a decision I took very soon after I wrote that essay. Clearly, I was trying to persuade myself, as much as anybody else, to leave university life. Nowadays, even though I still fundamentally believe in the premise of my essay, I would no longer take that high-handed moral tone.

GL: In this essay, you argue that the academic's poetry is "experience filtered through literature", and all of his gods are always perched on his shoulders. He also studies the pitfalls of his gods so well that his evasive measures turn to paralysis and his poetry says nothing. The result, is minor poetry at best.

AA: I suspect that this is less true now because nobody at university reads anything. They read theory; they don't actually read the text, the poetry. The scenario in which an academic writes a poem and thinks, "Donne would have done that better", is probably very unlikely these days.

GL: Are there any poets from the 1960s or 1970s who, although currently neglected, may be the gods of tomorrow?

AA: I don't know, but I question the gods of today. I'm glad Heaney won the Nobel because I think he's a very good poet. I do not think he's W.B. Yeats, and I've gone on record saying that. There is one terrible anomaly in the poetry world: there is no doubt in my mind that the world's greatest living poet is Zbigniew Herbert. The fact that he has not won a Nobel Prize is a disgrace.

GL: Let's expand on the earlier subject of Plath and public perceptions. How will *Birthday Letters* affect our perceptions of her, Ted, and their relationship?

AA: One of the things I learned when I was doing my book on divorce was that not only do people have different versions of what happens in a marriage, but they sometimes don't even agree about the basic *facts*. Everybody has their own marriage, as it were. Each makes a selection of the experience. It's been thirty-five years since Sylvia died. During all those years Ted has been thinking about it, grieving over it, trying to work out why this nightmare happened. He's not just been giving himself excuses, but finding a plot so that he can understand what happened. To use that terrible psychoanalytical term, he's been

"processing" it.

The subtext of a lot of the poems is also the main text of the Stevenson biography. And that is that Sylvia was seriously crazy – and had been since well before she met Ted. This may have been true, though how can any of us know? But this must be what Ted tells himself in order to understand what happened. You also have to realise that a lot of her late poems – her great poems – are very much about this break-up. They're made out of her daily life as she led it through this disaster. They comprise her story of it. But it's now been thirty-five years and it's enough. He's saying, "That was her version, here is mine".

GL: The story has been so lopsided, in her favour, because he has been silent. It has been: "Ted wronged Sylvia". What do you remember of those last months of their marriage and her life?

AA: When Ted left Sylvia he came and stayed with me for three days. And I'm fairly convinced that probably she first called on me to read me those wonderful *Ariel* poems for more than one reason. Yes, I was a poetry critic at the time – I was very much on that wavelength – so she knew that she would have the ear of someone who could listen. But also I think that she just wanted to sniff around to see where Ted had been. By that time, he had found himself somewhere else to live; he didn't tell me where; I didn't ask.

I was very much attuned to the kind of things she was writing: when my own marriage was breaking up I made a suicide attempt, a very serious one. This was one of the things Sylvia and I had in common. She knew I had been there. We were members of the same club, as it were. I think this is why she trusted me to read those poems. Now, I look back on that person I was and I don't even recognise him. No way would that ever happen again. And not just because I'm older and case-hardened, but because that's not how it works for me anymore.

It's perfectly possible to have a very bloody divorce and go through long periods of depression and grief and rage and all the things you're expected to go through in these harrowing circumstances and still not actually kill yourself. But especially because I've been there myself, I'm not even remotely suggesting that Sylvia's reaction was incomprehensible. But there seem to have been so many reasons for her not to go *that* far: above all, her children, whom she adored; also, the poems she was writing – they are full of life, and she knew how good they were. I'll tell you what I also got from *Birthday Letters*: a feeling that I've had well before reading the book is that if she had been able to play her cards at all – never mind play them right – that it mightn't have ended the way it did.

Although I was privy to a certain amount of their troubles, I did not put any of it in *The Savage God* because I actually felt that, in the immortal words of Robert Graves, "The problems of their marriage bed were none of our damn business". It didn't seem proper to write about this. They were going through a divorce; I had just been through a divorce. Divorces are awful experiences in which everybody behaves badly.

GL: Do you think that with *Birthday Letters* will come a new understanding of Ted as a person?

AA: Well, one hopes so. But that depends on who is doing the understanding. The unhinged feminists are going to stay unhinged. They're not suddenly going to drop all of their prejudices. It's not like the Iron Curtain coming down. A card-carrying feminist is a card-carrying feminist on that particular level, and probably will still have to see him as a villain.

GL: Maybe one good thing about *Birthday Letters* is that a monologue can now become a dialogue. Maybe that will redress a lot of wasted time and energy spent on this subject.

AA: Exactly. What seems to be striking about the collection is that a large number of them are love poems. He's been brooding on this for a long time. A little bit like Hardy who behaved terribly when his wife was alive and then wrote those heartbroken poems after her death. This is not unprecedented in the human psyche.

GL: How do you define "love" here? And how does it work with what seems to be a strong element of detachment – or the desire for it – in a number of the poems? In 'The Rabbit Catcher', he says, "I was a fly outside on the window-pane / Of my own domestic drama". In 'Karlsbad Caverns', he admires bats who, in their millions, turn back to their cave as a storm approaches: "Unlike us, / They knew how, and when, to detach themselves / from the love that moves the sun and other stars".

AA: Some are love poems in that they seem to me to be wracked with guilt and grief. I see this as attachment. But a lot of them, like 'The 59th Bear' and 'The Rabbit Catcher', are answers to things Sylvia had written. I am totally convinced that the people who are just interested in the "he done her wrong – she done him wrong" story aren't going to be satisfied, because in order to take full account of his poems you have to know her poetry quite well.

GL: The personal histories of Ted and Sylvia aside, what does *Birthday Letters* tell us about Ted's development as a poet?

AA: My feeling about this is that Ted found his voice very early on. It's there in his first volume, *The Hawk in the Rain* (1957). By his mid-twenties, he knew what turned him on. You've got poems like 'An Otter', 'Hawk Roosting', and 'The Thought-Fox'. As I said, he had that hotline open to his demons. Sylvia, however, while highly competent, was not yet in touch with her demons. She couldn't get through to the damn things. What Ted did was to help her get through. In 'The Minotaur', he writes about one of her rages at him. She smashes a mahogany table-top. He tells her: "That's the stuff you're keeping out of your poems!". He helped her to get in touch with her rage *as a poet* – and then all the demons came streaming out.

His particular means of getting through are not anything I particularly admire. There's a lot of mumbo-jumbo: the tarot pack, the ouija board, the dark gods. All that Lawrentian bullshit. But it worked. You have to understand the degree to which we were all totally brainwashed on the subject of D. H. Lawrence in the '50s. Lawrence nearly ruined my life. (I even married Frieda's granddaughter.) He was a very powerful figure.

So, Ted taught her how to get through to her demons. Because she'd served such a long apprenticeship, she had all the discipline and skill needed to cope once she faced them. He, on the other hand, from the fallout of this disaster disappeared into a long "off" period. *Crow* (1970) is a fine volume, but there are a lot of poems in the '60s and '70s that are pretty forget-

> [Hughes's] particular means of getting through are not anything I particularly admire. There's lots of mumbo-jumbo: the tarot pack, the ouija board, the dark gods. All that Lawrentian bullshit.

table. Great swathes of mediocrity. *Wodwo* (1967) is not a good book.

What is so curious about *Birthday Letters* is that, in some important way, Ted often sounds like Sylvia. In her early writing, she sounds like him only once. In 'Poem for a Birthday', in *The Colossus*, she's faintly fumbling towards her own voice and actually sounds like him. Then when she found her voice, she kind of overtook him. He had been the "wonderful" poet, but, in that final year, she became the "wonderful" one. If it hadn't been for that horrible final year, she'd have been a quite minor figure.

It's like Keats's penultimate year. (He was too ill to write in his final year.) All of his great poems follow the death of his brother, Tom – and they're all about death, the whole bloody lot of them. William Empson has a brilliant comment about the first line to 'Ode to Melancholy': "No, no, go not to Lethe, neither twist". Empson said that something in the poet's mind must have wanted to go to Lethe very badly if it took four negatives in the first line to stop him. If Keats hadn't written those death poems, he would've ended up a minor follower of Leigh Hunt. If Sylvia had died a year before she did, she would have remained relegated to the schools of Wallace Stevens and Ted Roethke. In her last year, all the poems are about rage, despair and abandonment: and she became a great poet.

In some of the better poems in *Birthday Letters*, you can see that Ted has learned from Sylvia. You can see her stylistic devices and hear her tone of voice. They had a very close marriage, and that's what happens: you pick up each other's strengths and weaknesses. You learn from each other. Their marriage happened to be fore-shortened, but this book shows that, on one level, it went on.

GL: Let's discuss your own poetry. *Autumn to Autumn and Selected Poems, 1953-1976* (1978) was your last collection. Have you continued to write and publish?

AA: I have published several poems in *The Sunday Times, The New Yorker* and other magazines, but nothing in book form. My problem has been that I have always thrown a lot of things away. Everything depends on finding your own voice. Once you've heard the way you want to sound, once it sounds to you as though you are speaking it, then you can do anything. I must have picked up this voice thing from Sylvia. She would never

let me read her poems. She would always say, "I want you to *hear* them". I think that this later helped me to change my voice to my true one, which I began to do in the *Autumn to Autumn* sequence, written in 1974 and 1975. One of the few earlier poems in which I manage to do it is called 'Mourning and Melancholia', one about the death of my father. I think that a lot of the earlier poems are about being unhappy.

GL: I wanted to ask you about just that. Your poems confront divorce, death, abortion, and other emotionally harrowing themes. The confessional and personal elements are deep and powerful. Your poems seem to be studies in catharsis: "transitions" are common – not depictions of the before and after, but in what seem to be "pivots" when consciousness records/accepts change: love to the death of love, one season to another, weather, night to day, dreaming to waking. Are these catharses?

AA: I don't know, that's a very interesting point; it's also interesting to hear someone else's take on it. I had a terribly, and mutually, unhappy first marriage. We were very nasty to each other. I wrote a lot of poems about that and other painful things and began to feel that I couldn't write anything unless I was unhappy. I think that the *Autumn to Autumn* sequence changed things. It's all about coming alive. I hope the poems I've written in recent years show this, too. In general, my later poetry is much more relaxed. What I actually do is write poetry, that's what I have always wanted to do, and I think of myself as a poet. But you don't make a living out of writing poetry and I've chosen to stay out of academia, in spite of having the qualifications. I've also managed to get out of the business of just making a living as a literary critic. I ended up writing a lot of different kinds of books.

GL: Do you think you protected your poetic self by leaving academia and ranging far and wide in your writing?

AA: I am sure that real poetry only comes from a live core, a real voice, which one finds by living living as freely as you are able. Drawn from elsewhere, poetry is slightly confected. I've always believed that we have only one shot at this planet, and I'd like to try as much as I can of what it has to offer. Besides doing a lot of different things in my life, what has also helped is that I've usually been broke. That has kept me writing, kept me hungry, kept up the tension.

Genealogies

by Gillian Allnutt

FLEUR ADCOCK

Looking Back

Oxford Poets, £6.99
ISBN 019288068 5

JULIAN STANNARD

**Fleur Adcock In Context
From Movement to Martians**

The Edwin Mellen Press
Volume 29 in the series Studies in
British Literature, £39.95
ISBN 0 7754 8687 9
SBL Series ISBN 0 88946 927 X

THERE'S A NICE symmetry to *Looking Back*. In the first part we meet Adcock's ancestors — backwards, as one traces one's ancestors — from the mill-hands of Manchester in the 1890s to the dubious men banging about the early 14th Century court of Edward II. In the second part, where all the poems are personal and many autobiographical, we move among the living generations of the family, beginning with Adcock's childhood and ending in the company of her 90-year-old mother and, in 'The Video', that lovely vignette of sibling rivalry, of her own granddaughters:

Ceri played
the video again and again.
She watched Laura come out, and then,
in reverse, she made her go back in.

I found myself absorbed in Adcock's ancestors, poring over the (brief) notes at the back, trying to get the lineage straight in my mind; more absorbed, indeed, than I have ever been in my own genealogy. That, of course, is because Adcock is no ego-bound bore of a relation anxious to show off the results of relentless research, but a poet able to poke fun at herself (and us) for undertaking the business in the first place. Here she is looking for the burial plaque of one Griffith Hampden (1543-1591) and his wife Anne Cave:

Well, then, says the vicar,

it will be under the carpets:
a brass...
He rolls the strip of red carpet;
I roll the underfelt.
It sheds fluff.

('At Great Hampden')

Indeed, it may be that Adcock's sharp, often deflationary humour has been handed down from the ancestors themselves. Great-great-great-uncle Francis Eggington, back from the Crimea and asked "what's that hole inside your beard?", has a flash of prophetic insight:

"Tea first" he said. "I'll tell you later.
And Willie's children will tell their grandchildren;
I'll be a thing called oral history."

('The Russian War')

Three poems concern the turning up of the late 16th/early 17th Century Frances St John. 'Beanfield' begins in "right idiot" mode — "Somehow you've driven fifty miles to stand / in a beanfield ..." — but ends quite differently:

She's here; she's not here; she was once.
The larks are other larks' descendants.
Four hundred years. It feels like a kind of love.

At once the briskly practice Frances challenges this with "What are you loving me with? I'm dead" and later declares:

What's left of me, if you gathered it up,
is a faggot of bones, some ink-scrawled paper,
flown-away cells of skin and hair...

('Ancestor to Devotee')

She has a point. And yet curiosity alone could not have made a woman out of these remains. It has to be love, a kind of love, that allows her to come to life and speak for herself, partly through her will, quoted here, and partly through the medium of Adcock's attentive imagination

Item I give to my sonne Samuell Browne
my halfe dozen of silver spoones
They've had quite a history, those spoons.
My first husband bequeathed them to my second

('Frances')

Almost my favourite ancestor has the final word.

Peter Wentworth, MP, 1524-1597, was imprisoned in the Tower of London several times by Elizabeth I for demanding that Parliament should be free to discuss the succession and other matters without interference. But it isn't that. It's just that Austen herself could not have produced a more perfectly English man – and it's all in the way of putting it:

> My Pithie Exhortation still exists – go and read it in your British Library. I have discussed it here with your father; he was always a supporter of free speech.
> ('Peter Wentworth in Heaven')

'The Pilgrim Fathers' (no Adcock relations, these) was the title of "my first public poem, when I was nine" and is that of a poem here that has a gentle go at the lit crit industry. When she was nine, "no one probed into my influences, / or said 'Miss Adcock, perhaps you could explain // your position as regards colonialism'". Possibly the genesis of this poem lies partly in Adcock's experience of providing "useful information" to Julian Stannard who has written the first full-length study of her work. *Fleur Adcock in Context* is subtitled "From Movement to Martians" and provides an object lesson in literary genealogy. Written in an academic context and prefaced by Stannard's supervisor,

Michael Wood, the study is orthodox, straightforward. It traces the line of development in post-war British poetry from Larkin and The Movement in the Fifties through The Group/Workshop in the early Sixties to the Morrison/Motion *Penguin Book of Contemporary British Poetry* published in 1982 and on to the work of Christopher Reid and Michael Hofmann as exemplars of a younger generation. Stannard looks at Adcock's work as a response to and individual variation on the successive dicta of poetic practice in these post-war years. He has a chapter called "Other Forms of Protest: The Problem With Men". The problem, for me, with this study, this poetic genealogy, is the predictable absence of any Pilgrim Mothers.

And the presentation. Why is it that, in a culture that appears to value the "virtual reality" of presentation more than the "reality" of content, books fare so badly? Not only is this one barely proofed – though I admit that finding myself listed in the bibliography as "Galleon Allnutt" gave a lift to my sails – it suffers also from basic errors of grammar and punctuation. I find this unforgivable in a study of one of the most meticulous of contemporary British poets.

The Edwin Mellen Press, Lampeter, Dyfed SA48 7DY

The Unclassifiable Kobold

by Paul Groves

JOHN HEATH-STUBBS

Galileo's Salad
Carcanet, £7.95
ISBN 1 85754 260 6

The Torriano Sequences
Hearing Eye, £9.99
ISBN 1 870841 50 6

IT IS IMPOSSIBLE to dislike *Galileo's Salad*; impossible also to believe that its creator is blind, for the book fizzes with light, life, and acute description. If a third impossibility may be allowed, it is the reali-

sation that John Heath-Stubbs is eighty; the pages are aglitter with youthful high spirits. He presents a moving target ("I... will not be classified"), swinging from erudition to near-doggerel, sometimes in the same poem: 'Balaeniceps Rex' asks "Why do I write this stuff? My muse / Inclines at present to refuse, / And when that lady needs a stand-in, / Writing mere verse can keep one's hand in".

Kobolds are mischievous household sprites found in German mythology. His use of the term could be self-descriptive, as a corresponding humour infuses the collection. In the sparkling 'The King of the Cats', dedicated to the memory of George Barker, the author panders the literary scene: "What I mostly see is a litter of kittens, / Who handle poetry with woolly mittens; / They chase their own tails, they worry small rats – / But where's the undoubted king of the cats?" One could contend, with some justification, that John Heath-Stubbs is just such a creature. Others may object that he is locked into a scholarly realm to which entrants are barred by such terms as "Troynovant", "fanglement", "protending", "lucifuge", and "sprig-gans", none of which are in the average dictionary; "ophicleide" may be, but how many know it was a wind instrument played by Queen Victoria's husband – or, as the poet might insist, Albert Francis Charles Augustus Emmanuel of Saxe-Coburg-Gotha? Just as we swoon with lexical fatigue, he trills: "Mid-Lent, and Mothering Sunday's come – / A bunch of dates for good old Mum".

At least Heath-Stubbs is consistent, in that he has always displayed literary legerdemain. His style has developed less than might have been expected, which suggests that he found his voice early and has rarely wavered. It is a reassuringly positive voice: "the vast yawn of the godless universe" in 'A Great Cosmic Cheer' is belied by the title, whose optimism echoes and re-echoes throughout the book. Although, to use a phrase from 'Balakirev and the Bugs', there is a good deal of "Detailed, pedantic knowledge" here, this can seem preferable to street-wise philistinism. His leaning towards antiquity could be our problem, not his. He classifies the English thus: "– that race, as someone said, / Born always two stiff drinks below par". *Galileo's Salad* is the work of a writer who knows no such handicap.

The Torriano Sequences, illustrated hauntingly by Emily Johns, is in six sections: 'Cats' Parnassus', 'Time Pieces', 'A Partridge in a Pear Tree', 'A Ninefold of Charms', 'The Parson's Cat', and 'Chimaeras'. These are not throwaway titles: the contents strictly adhere to the themes. Many are first-rate: 'Inscription for a Sundial' and 'Egg-Timer', for example, have a faultless tone. Others tend too easily towards the jokily conversational; the ending of 'Against a Rat' is schoolboyishly silly: "I'll bandy no more verses with you, you git – So just git!" Thankfully, such shortcomings are rare. Mostly you are in the presence of a clubbable old don, who provides good company and "warmth,

security, English comfort" ('The Parson's Cat Is A Homely Cat'). Some critics might bridle at Heath-Stubbs's relentlessly didactic tone and love of esotery: how many poets could get away with 'Batrachomyomachia' and "Lavolta, piedz-en-l'air and saltarello, / Trepaks and gopaks?" But the writer doesn't mind who he offends, for he is clearly enjoying himself. Many pieces would read well to an audience, and Heath-Stubbs, the canny old trouper, knows it. If you can accommodate someone who compares the side of a bath to "the Leucadian cliff, / That Sappho leapt from" or who says of a classroom clock "Euclid of Megara might have seen beauty there" and who, with unshakeable self-confidence, writes of a lion falling in love with an ant (moreover, "their love was consummated"), then Heath-Stubbs is your man. If, however, these clever-boy antics pall after a few pages, you might turn to less ambitious lines by less accomplished practitioners. It is only then that you will miss the overall richness of the working, the old-fashioned and newfangled lying side by side as incongruous but ultimately appealing bedfellows. It is for this unique blend of learning, loquacity, and liveliness that Heath-Stubbs has a loyal band of followers, whose number – if these books have anything to do with it – will grow rather than diminish. If you should wonder whether to join them, read 'Five Gold Rings': in my notebook I commented "superb, because immediate and tactile; pure crafts-manship". I was not tempted to cross this out in case it sounded excessively laudatory, for – in the same sequence 'Nine Ladies Dancing' elicited a similar response. Part of the writer's success derives from his sure ear; this is not only attributable to his sightlessness but to a musicality which derives from his mother, a professional pianist. Anyone addicted to the allure of youth for youth's sake in British poetry should be mindful of what they are missing among the works of this most likeable of poets.

Glass Eyelids

by Moniza Alvi

IMTIAZ DHARKER
Postcards From God

Bloodaxe, £8.95
ISBN 1 85224 4070

A SYMBOL FOR Imtiaz Dharker's stance as a poet can be found in her poem '6 December 1992' which begins "This morning I woke / and found my eyelids / turned to glass". Her clear-sighted alertness to the extremities of a culture, her refusal not to see, pervades this collection. Imtiaz Dharker was born in Pakistan in 1954, grew up in Scotland and now lives in India. These transitions in her life have lent a sense of dislocation, allowing her to view cultural issues sharply, both as an insider and an outsider. The poet's drawings, included in this volume, emphasise the essential unity of her vision. The ramshackle houses and expressive faces lead inward to her concern with the spiritual and with human vulnerability in her artwork and her poetry.

The 'Postcards From God' section in this book is particularly striking. The poet speaks through the voice of a very human, alienated god who becomes a perfect vehicle for her exploration of the human condition. 'Postcards from god I' introduces this god as an entity forced to wander like a tourist through streets that have lost their promise. The desire to communicate is still there – thus god writes postcards, though it's not clear to whom. Their purpose is touchingly "Proof that I was here". The symbol of the eye appears on one of these postcards:

> Between the video walls and my face is the eye
> made in the inverted image
> of the unfinished sky.
> a slit where the unexplained looks through
> ('Postcards from god II')

This eye is the poet's watchfulness. It is one of the disturbing pictures that will be sent out, along with the prophetic "faces / that will belong to you / years from now, / waiting to be lived in, lined". From this sequence it is clear that the poet inhabits the modern world, the world of tradition, and a timeless world of human suffering and possibility.

The impoverished, rickety dwelling becomes, for Dharker, a symbol for human struggle. This symbolism is also found in the colonial/post-colonial novel. Naipaul's Mr Biswas continually searches for a suitable, secure home, and constantly finds himself in inferior houses. Kuttappen, in Arundhati Roy's The God of Small Things, wonders what people who had more than four corners in their houses did with the rest of their corners. In the short poem 'Living Space' the poet describes a hovel: "The whole structure leans dangerously towards the miraculous". The partly humorous use of "miraculous" is subtle preparation for a quizzically transcendent ending – hanging from this shaky home are some white eggs in a wire basket "gathering the light / into themselves, / as if they were / the bright, thin walls of faith". More obliquely in the intricate 'Shell', an egg is about to hatch a fragile dwelling. First the poet offers a straightforward close-up of "a tulsi plant in a Dalda tin", and the protective "mirchi and lemon over the door". Then her penetrating gaze, both realistic and visionary reveals: "all

the lives show through / the boards and beams / that might as well / be paper, glass".

The strength of the 'Postcards From God' series lies partly in the poet's lightness of touch. Other poems in this Bloodaxe collection have different strengths, though they work best when Dharker's passionate voice combines with a subtlety of approach. 'Another Woman' presents forcefully the tragic plight of a powerless woman. She couldn't afford the luxury of a white radish, "just imagined the crunch it would make / between her teeth, the sharp, sweet taste". The radish and the preparation of food seem to stand for pleasures absent from a life in which she has had no real choice:

> This was the house she had been sent to,
> the man she had been bound to,
> the future she had been born into.

Her only choice is to die by the fire she has observed as "a wing of brightness" beating against the "blackened cheek" of an old pot. It is a difficult subject for poetry, but Dharker avoids the purely polemical through her physical grounding of the poem and her imaginative insights. 'Purdah I' also focuses on a woman who is exiled from herself. The poet combines anger with a sense of the hidden and mystical. She begins ironically: "One day they said / she was old enough to learn some shame. / She found it came quite naturally". Irony turns to outrage as the woman's garment is described as covering her in the same way earth falls on a coffin. The effects of purdah are insidious: "We sit still, / letting the cloth grow / a little closer to our skin".

Fittingly, the alienation in 'Purdah I' is echoed in the final poem, 'Minority', where the poet portrays herself as a foreigner, even where her relatives are buried "their fingers and faces pushing up / new shoots of maize and sugarcane". Writing is her release and makes communication possible. It is also her right: "Everyone has the right / to infiltrate a piece of paper". Hope is apparent, for example in the liveliness of creativity, as expressed in 'Making the Angels':

> A host of fledgling angels, spat
> like grape-seed, out
> of a newmade, unsuspecting sky.

Imtiaz Dharker's poetry is brave and far-reaching. She makes a welcome and very significant contribution to the literature of exile.

IN APPRECIATION OF

Denise Levertov (1923–1998)

by Elaine Feinstein

DENISE LEVERTOV WAS born on 24 October 1923 in Iford, Essex She left this country for the United States in 1948 as a G.I bride, and her poetry developed under the influence of Ezra Pound, William Carlos Williams and Charles Olson. She came to be regarded as an altogether American poet, and always enjoyed a more powerful presence on the American scene than on this side of the Atlantic.

Levertov had a true lyric gift She used little imagery, and the music of her lines lay in their phrasing, their disposition on the page following the breath of a human voice, as she had learned from Black Mountain poets. Her most characteristic early poems make the physical world about her numinous in and of itself; a domestic world perhaps, but never tame. She writes of

Photograph by Chris Felver

> This wild night gathering
> > the washing as if it were flowers
> animal vines twisting over the line and
> slapping my face lightly, soundless merriment
> in the gesticulation of shirtsleeves,
> I recall out of my joy a night of misery.

Our literary paths often crossed. In 1959 I published a poem of hers about lemon trees in my short-lived magazine *Prospect*, and we corresponded for a time. It may be because we share Russian Jewish roots that we have occasionally written poems on similar topics; indeed, at the time I was working on Marina Tsvetayeva, she was too,

unknown to me, translating five lyrics from that great Russian poet.

As the child of a Jewish mother and a Methodist Minister, her inheritance was a more complex one, and her search for a spiritual dimension in her life led her to investigate native American wisdom, the Kabbalah, and other forms of mysticism.

In the early 'eighties, we met in Toronto, at Harbourfront. It was at the time of the Irish hunger strikes, and Bobby Sands had died a few days earlier. I remember how warmly she greeted John Montague with a hug of sympathy. Her political commitment was always generous, even though it did not feed her lyric impulse; her hatred of digging uranium out of the earth to make bombs, her opposition to War in Vietnam, her loathing of American Imperialism, were always heartfelt expressions of her human warmth. And she never lost the ability to give radiance to the ordinary. In her early books there is often a marital bed, where a couple drowse "mouth-to-mouth" in the shared warmth, while by day they "are singular and often lonely". Looking at her wedding ring many years later, after divorce, she sees it lying

> among keys to abandoned houses
> nails waiting to be needed and hammered

and wishes to have it transformed into a less unlucky gift for others, which could never be taken

for solemn betrothal or to make promises
living will not let them keep.

Her death came as a complete surprise. She was exuberant, direct and when I last saw her, in Paris, looked twenty years younger than her physical age. Hearing she had died suddenly, I remembered the marvellous poem for her mother facing a "laggard death" with bed sores, incontinent, with a plastic tube taped to her nose. I could never be brave enough to say myself, as Levertov does in a verse from that poem:

> O Lord of mysteries, how beautiful is sudden death
> when the spirit vanishes
> boldly and without casting
> a single shadowy feather of hesitation

on to the felled body.

Denise Levertov, who always lived with nerve, had the courage to say and mean it. Levertov held a number of prestigious teaching posts: at Vassar College, University of California at Berkeley, and Massachusetts Institute of Technology, Cambridge. She also won a number of literary prizes, among them a Guggenheim Fellowship and two American Academy grants. From 1980, Levertov was a member of the American Academy. Her husband Mitchell Goodman was also a writer, and it was through him that she met many of the poets of the Beat generation including Allen Ginsberg. They had one son; their divorce was finalised in 1975. She will be much missed by all those who knew her and listened to her poems.

Jon Silkin (1930–1997)

by Rodney Pybus

THE SUDDEN DEATH of Jon Silkin late last November, a week before his 67th birthday, could hardly have come at a crueller moment. He had finally admitted to himself and others that it really was time to look for someone younger and fresher to take over *Stand* Magazine. He always did the work of ten, and in that sense as well as in terms of originating vision he is irreplaceable. But there is no reason why the magazine should not continue. The search is on for a new editor and that person will no doubt put his or her own stamp on it, so this is an appropriate time to reflect on *Stand* under Jon Silkin's editorship, and to appreciate his achievement as a poet.

He founded it 45 years ago to "take a stand" against apathy and conformism – political, social and aesthetic; and to promote the belief that human beings can change and grow morally. The belief, if you like, that paradise can be regained. For Jon these commitments were all part of what it meant to be a serious human being, and he held to them fervently throughout his long career as poet, critic, editor and teacher. The early 1950s was also the period when he was writing the poems that went into *The Peaceable Kingdom*, his first collection which Cecil Day Lewis published at Chatto and

Windus in 1954. This remains an extraordinary achievement, one of the great debut volumes in its mature lyrical voice, its passionate bodying forth of what became his abiding themes of our place in nature, love and death, our inhumanity towards ourselves and other creatures, and of course Jewishness.

His *Selected Poems* (Routledge, 1980) reprints about half of them, but it's a pity most readers can't have easy access to all of that first volume – not just the famous 'Death of a Son' but 'The three birds who were saints', 'The cunning of an age' and 'No land like it'. The latter two are "fox poems", anticipating Ted Hughes and (naturally) his younger *Stand* co-editor of the early sixties, Ken Smith. 'No land like it' begins "My country is a fox's country / With moors of drenching sunlight and olive trees, / And peace hanging from the branches in clusters of birds / There is no other country like it". One can catch faint echoes in these early poems of some of his early influences: D.H. Lawrence, Isaac Rosenberg, maybe Dylan Thomas (who, after all, had died only in 1953), the Old Testament of the James Bible (perhaps at a deeper level Milton and Wordsworth – if he'd had to choose one desert island poet I think it might well have been

Wordsworth). But he found a distinctive voice from the start and, while it changed, you could never confuse a Silkin poem with anyone else's.

It's often said that the period when both Silkin and *Stand* were at their very best and absolutely central to British literary life was from the early 1960s through to perhaps the end of the 1970s. A cursory look through issues from that time would show that the magazine published new poetry and prose by, among many other important writers, Beckett, Sartre, Pinter, Neruda, Ginsberg, Geoffrey Hill, Tony Harrison, Seamus Heaney, Douglas Dunn, Christopher Middleton, Michael, Hamburger, Roy Fisher, Joseph Brodsky, Alan Sillitoe, Angela Carter, Peter Carey, Charles Tomlinson, R. S. Thomas, Peter Redgrove, MacDiarmid, Randolph Stow, Norman Nicholson, Jeffrey Wainwright, and from the United States such as Philip Levine, James Merrill, G.P. Elliott, William Stafford, Mark Strand, Robert Bly, and so on. Even this only nods to one of the magazine's central preoccupations, new work in translation – from Russia, all over Eastern Europe, Latin America, Scandinavia etc. Indisputably this was a matchless line-up.

It's arguable that among British magazines of the 1990s *Stand* has not looked quite so central. My own feeling is that this impression arises from the fact that, while *Stand*'s fundamental concerns haven't changed, their context has. We live in a less concerned, less serious, less optimistic, less committed society, for which literature itself may be less central. In the same way, Jon himself felt that over the last decade he had not been at the centre of things as a poet. While part of him knew that his *oeuvre* had very few challengers among living poets, another part of him wondered why, if this were indeed the case, more people didn't seem to recognise and acknowledge it. The style was the man to an unusual degree – complex, elusive, intellectually dense and gritty, rich and passionate. He never swerved, never abandoned his big themes, never wrote a "light" or a trivial poem, never re-modelled himself for the sake of reputation or reader.

His reputation may have suffered because his tactics from, say, *Amana Grass* (1971) onwards had less and less to do with the "plain style" of the heirs to The Movement and Larkin that characterised much of English writing in his lifetime. If he was sometimes excessively obscure and contorted, this at least reflected and enacted the authentic tensions and existential struggles that were going on within. No doubt there will be, one day, a *Collected Poems*, but in the meantime I wish those unfamiliar with his poetry could come freshly, with an open mind, to the splendidly Lawrentian nature poems, the political and social concerns of his 'Killhope Wheel' sequence from the early '70s, the tangled lyricism of the 'Urban Psalms', the cheerily unflinching honesty of the 'Autobiographical Stanzas'. More than enough riches there for anyone, surely.

And for all he was a famously difficult man I am very glad to have been his friend and literary colleague in different ways for most of my adult life. Perhaps he was in the end too unEnglish, not quite one of "our team" with his discomfiting, impassioned intensity. Given his Russian-Jewish background, there's no earthly reason why he should have ended up as another straight-up-and-down suburban ironist. My own belief is that Jon Silkin's voice and vision will come eventually to be seen as one of the most enriching and substantial poetic achievements of the second half of this century. If I'm wrong, so much the worse for us. For the moment I console myself with the final stanza of his 'Epilogue' to *The Peaceable Kingdom*:

Photograph by Philip Rutter

If all the people and all the animals
Joined dark with light, if all the proud people
And soft-stepping circus climbed their way in the
                                        dark
Walked with the black seals and walked with the
                                        spidery flies
They would all go into the great light, and they
                                        would know.

NEWS/COMMENT

SOMETHING WE HAVE GOT THAT THEY DON'T

University College, London, is holding a major conference on Anglo-American poetic relations from July 9th to 11th. Organised by Mark Ford and Steve Clark, the conference includes readings by John Ashbery and Jorie Graham, lectures by Helen Vendler and Marjorie Perloff, and features John Bayley on Larkin, Berryman and Lowell, Ian Sansom on the American Auden, Michael Donaghy on 'The Anglophobia of the American Poet', Stephen Burt on Michael Hofmann and Lowell, Tim Kendall on Sylvia Plath and almost 80 futher talks. The conference is sponsored by the *TLS* which will be producing an American issue. **Booking details from Steve Clarke, fax: 0171 436 4533.**

NET VERSE

When I reviewed the Literature Online site at **http://lion.chadwyck.co.uk/** in the last *Poetry Review*, there wasn't anything available unless you paid up. They've now added some worthwhile free resources, including a searchable database of 1000 love poems, and a lively masterclass, workshop and discussion group run by Matthew Sweeney which are well worth a visit.

CompuServe is another institution that's offering limited free access. They've provided Web access to many of their forums, including the Poetry Forum at **http://www.csi.com/go_c.asp? PIN=Poetry** and non-members can access some of the sections to find out what goes on there. I have to declare an interest here, since they've just made me one of the senior sysops of the place, but I reckon it's still the best place on-line for poetry discussions and workshops. Opinions vary as to whether the limited access to non-members is sufficient to be interesting rather than frustrating, but it's probably worth a look.

A light-hearted, but beautifully presented site is Claire Schaeffer's Wocky Jivvy. Navigate to **http://www.wockyjivvy.com/** for an archive of some famous poems, given an added twist with some off-beat graphics. Great fun. Also check out Claire's monthly poetry quiz, and her increasingly desperate attempts not to be selected as an NLP semifinalist.

http://www3.sympatico.ca/ray.saitz/poetry.htm

is a site without a title. What it does have are some extremely useful essays and lessons on poetry, and links to other sites with similar stuff. If you're teaching or studying poetry, it's a must. BigBear Publications is a relatively small Small Press outfit. Its relatively small site at **http://www.bigbear.u-net.com/** is currently excited about the imminent release of its latest publication: a collection of poems by Steve Anderson about Mother Shipton. There are enough examples of the work to let you know if you want to fork out for it.

If you know of a good site, let me know about it via: peter@hphoward.demon.co.uk

LETTERS

DUTCH ISSUES

Dear Peter,

I am growing a little weary of being hectored in your Letters columns about the wonders of Dutch poetry. Ms. Deborah Ffoulkes (*PR*, Vol 87 No 3, p.95) felt short-changed by the space allocated to my review of James Brockway's *Singers Behind Glass: Eight Modern Dutch Poets* (Vol 87 No 2, p.68). Her comment that "At only 44 column centimetres I really do not feel I am getting value for money" was the only part of her letter which could be described as measured. A letter which outrageously speculates that a dead poet, Gerrit Achterberg – praised in my review (and affirmatively reviewed by me elsewhere in the past) – might "have slapped a fatwah on O'Driscoll for slandering the poetic achievement of this tiny but mighty literary nation" deserves simply to be forwarded to *Index on Censorship*.

Had Mr Victor Schiferli of the Foundation for the Production and Translation of Dutch Literature (Vol 87 No 4, p.95) read my review as carefully as I read Brockway's anthology, he would not have asserted that I was judging Dutch poetry "on the basis of one small selection of a translator's eight favourite poets". Short though my review was, it listed – for starters – a further nine modern Dutch poets with whose work I am well acquainted. Among the poets I named was Judith Herzberg (I have not only read her work in magazines and in her Oberlin selection, but have met her and heard her read). Yet Mr Schiferli includes her in his most bizarre of categories: "outstanding poets I trust

Dennis O'Driscoll has never heard about".

I admit to further breaches of Mr Schiferli's "trust" by having presumed to read several of the other poets on his list. I have also collaborated with a Dutch scholar on translations of a number of poets, Gerrit Achterberg not least; most of these have been published, one was used on Dublin's equivalent of *Poems on the Underground*. Notwithstanding Mr Schiferli's inference to the contrary, therefore, I have surely earned the right to express 44 centimetres worth of opinion on Dutch poetry at this stage. If, however, he believes that I have not, then my assiduous reading of publications which his Foundation supported has been a waste of time.

Yours sincerely,

DENNIS O'DRISCOLL

County Kildare

Ireland

PANIC ATTACK

Dear Editor,

I was alarmed by Gillian Allnutt's panic at my current collection *Swimming Through The Grand Hotel* (Vol 87 No 4, p.84). She says that my poems panic her because she is doesn't understand them. Oh dear. What a dainty form of panning.

Gillian Allnutt goes through two poems at length to explain her loss of nerve – this takes up most of the review. She goes through another two shortly, one of which, about Israel/Palestine, she says she cannot really praise, because she does not know enough about the place. Damn, I should have included an Op Ed from the *Guardian*. But she says she loves its imagery anyway. So why look the little gift horse... In a world which contains Ashbery and many an other, No Way am I an obscure poet. Example? 'Riff' kindly printed below the review by *PR* could not be considered by anyone baffling. Maybe Allnutt hasn't heard of the Mississippi.

Gillian is most completely mystified by my poem 'A photograph seen when I was twelve'. This poem which audiences keep telling me they particularly like, must obviously be getting the critical goat on some wildly confused level for it has already attracted the wrath of a youthful reviewer elsewhere not for obscurity but for the rather different crime of "authorial intrusion" (What about "reviewer intrusion"?) In truth the poem is a serious attempt, based on certain obvious dramatic and metaphoric devices, to explore the very delicate matter of pornography and the Holocaust (and the Jewish English playwright and theatre director Julia Pascal immediately saw it for what it is and so did *The Honest Ulsterman* who originally published it – so there's a spread of interest for you). Gillian Allnutt's own bafflement finally comes down to rest on two words "till" and "store" which she (not I) thinks are anachronistic and therefore render the whole poem meaningless. Gee. Actually I thought poets dealt in the whole lot, meaning, language, metaphor, rhythms, image, observation, context, general cultural whatsits... But Gillian gives one sentence to a poem she did enjoy. Thank *you* Ma'am.

Genuine appraisal is harder work than knocking. But unfair reviewing where the good gets short shrift and the bad gets long, is a waste of everybody's time. Nor is it any good to say, you shouldn't care. Show me a poet who doesn't.

Yours sincerely,
JUDITH KAZANTZIS
London

SOME CONTRIBUTORS

Dick Allen's *Ode to the Cold War: Poems New and Selected* was published in America by Sarabande in 1997.
Stephen Burt's poetry will be included in Carcanet's *New Poetries 2*.
Killarney Clary's *Who Whispered Near Me* was published by Bloodaxe in 1993.
Billy Collins's latest collection is *The Art of Drowning* (University of Pittsburgh Press, 1995).
Mark Doty's new collection, *Sweet Machine*, will be published by Cape in June.
Elaine Feinstein's *Selected Poems* are published by Carcanet.
Lawrence Ferlinghetti will be appearing at the Brighton Festival on May 16.
John Greening's *New and Selected Poems* are due from Rockingham this year.
Ian Gregson's *Contemporary Poetry and Postmodernism: Dialogue and Estrangement* was published by Macmillan in 1996.
Emily Grosholz is currently Visiting Fellow at Clare Hall, Cambridge; her fourth collection, *The Abacus of Years*, will be published in 1999.
Marilyn Hacker's *Selected Poems* are published by Norton.
Anthony Hecht's latest collection is *Flight Among the Tombs* (OUP).
Mark Halliday's latest collection is *Tasker Street* (University of Massachusetts Press, 1992).
Brain Henry is an editor of *Verse*.
John Hollander's *The Work of Poetry (essays)* was published by Columbia University Press last year.
James Keery's first collection, *That Stranger, The Blues*, was published by Carcanet in 1997.
Anthony Julius's *T. S. Eliot, Anti-Semitism and Literary Form* is published by Cambridge University Press.
Mark Levine's poem in this issue is the title poem of his next collection, *Enola Gay*.
E. A. Markam's latest book is *Misapprehensions* (Anvil, 1992).
Ian McMillan's latest collection is *Dad, the Donkey's On Fire* (Carcanet).
Sandra McPherson's latest collection is *The Spaces between Birds* (Wesleyan University Press, 1996).
Stanley Moss's *Asleep in the Garden: New and Selected Poems* was published by Anvil this spring.
Julie O'Callaghan's latest collection is *Two Barks* (Bloodaxe).
Dennis O'Driscoll's latest collection is *Quality Time* (Anvil).
Rodney Pybus is an editor of *Stand*.
Justin Quinn is an editor of *Metre*.
Carol Rumens's *The Miracle Diet* was published by Bloodaxe in 1997.
William Scammell's new collection *All Set to Fall Off the Edge of the World* will be published by Flambard in June.
Gerald Stern's latest collection is *Odd Mercy* (Norton, 1995).
Anne Stevenson's *Collected Poems* are published by OUP.
David Wheatley's first collection, *Thirst*, is just out from Gallery.
C. D. Wright's next collection, *Deepstep Come Shining*, will be published by Copper Canyon in the Fall.
Andrew Zawacki is an editor of *Verse*.

ACKNOWLEDGMENT

With special thanks to Stephen Burt for his invaluable help in putting us in touch with American poets.